BHOJA RAJA

Idol of Sarasvatī, enshrined in Bhōja's temple of Śāradā (College).

BHOJA RAJA

P. T. SRINIVASA AYYANGAR

Published by

Facsimile Publisher
12 Pragati Market
Ashok Vihar, Ph-2
Delhi-110052
facsimilepublisher.com

Distribution Network
gyanbooks.com
India, USA, Canada, UK, Australia, France

ISBN : 978-93-5324-531-3 (HB)
First Published, Madras, 1931

2nd Impression 2020

Printed at: Gyan Press, Delhi.

Bhoja Raja

Author: P. T. Srinivasa Ayyangar

Dedicated to

Raja Sir S. R. M. Annamalai Chettiar, Kt.,

of Chettinad,

Founder of the Annamalai University.

FOREWORD.

This book was to have been only the first of a long series of historical studies which the late Professor P. T. Srinivas Ayyangar had contemplated for publication under the auspices of the Annamalai University. Unfortunately it has proved also his last. Death has too soon snatched him away from us, and we are left with only one memorial to his association with this University.

Prof. P. T. Srinivas Ayyangar's versatile intellect, his rare powers of discrimination, the thoroughness of his method and his command of the English language are so well known in these parts of the country that it is needless for me to expatiate on them. I may however be permitted to say that in this book we have a superb example of the kind of work we always associated with him. Inscriptions, tradition, literature have all been pressed into service, and the unique picture of Bhoja Raja of Dhārā stands out in bold relief against a background of Eleventh Century India which he has succeeded in painting so graphically. I can only wish that Indian historians followed this method oftener than they do at present.

Prof. P. T. Srinivas Ayyangar had asked me to go over the proofs of this book, and, being pressed for time, I had excused myself to him. Is it not a curious coincidence, then, that I should at last be called upon to do something for this book which he would have very much liked me to do?

ANNAMALAINAGAR
29th July, 1931.

K. M. KHADYE.

CONTENTS.

BHŌJA

CHAPTER I

MĀLVA

The Āḍābala hills, anglicized into the Arāvallis, and called the Pāriyātra mountains in the pre-Christian centuries, form the oldest mountain range of India, very much older than the Himālayas. They divide Rājaputāna, the home of the chivalrous Rājaputs, into two parts. One part comprises the great desert of India, which lies to the North-west of the Arāvallis; it is the bed of a great primæval sea, now dried up and overlaid with hills of blown sand fifty to hundred feet high. Over it sail the clouds of the South-west monsoon without parting with a drop of their precious burden; hence there is little vegetation and but one river, the Lūni, in this region. Separated from it by the Arāvallis lies South Rājaputāna, which is a part of the basin of the Ganges. Here

> "the ancient Rājaput dynasties rose to a position of pre-eminence among the dynasties of the continent. The sand-drifted landscapes of the northern regions of Rājaputāna are not wholly wanting to the south of the Arāvallis. . . . Wind-blown sand always lies conspicuous on the northern slopes of the long straight lines of rocky ridge which, south of the Arāvallis for many a league, indicates the ancient existence of a yet wider mountain system. Yet further south and east, the desert aspects of Rājaputāna are lost, merged in the comparatively fertile forest-clad highlands of peninsular India. But it is the Arāvallis that mark the line of division. Beyond them to the North-west lie the Indus and the tertiary flats which the Indus divides. South of them are ancient red-sandstone strata of the continent, and a region of broad open valleys and gentle slopes, with rivers flowing in permanent channels, magnificent forests, a comparatively even rainfall and temperate climate."[1]

---

[1] Imp. Gaz. Ind. i. pp. 34–35.

The highest point of the Arāvallis is called the Arbuda, ordinarily Mount Abū, where according to legend, some of the Rājaput families arose out of the fire-pit of Ṛṣi Vasiṣṭha, as will be related later. Of Mount Abu thus sang a poet-prince of Mālva and descendant of King Bhōja about eight hundred years ago:—

> "Well-known is the glorious mountain Arbuda (Ābū); it utterly humbles the pride of the noblest of mountains; the splendid colour which spreads from its sapphire crest, rivals that of the sky; on its top, which pierces the heaven, there are pools in which the lotus flower swings to and fro, and from it, pollen drops down and forms a circle, as if it were another vault of the sky. One end of the hill pierces the round orb of the earth which is girt with the ocean; the other pierces the sphere of heaven which ends in the circle of the horizon; hence this mountain looks like the glorious axle of the chariot of the Universe, one side of which lies down broken, on the rugged road, while the other is lifted upwards." [1]

Let us climb to the top of this Arbuda, very nearly four thousand feet above sea-level and turn our gaze to the south. Our eyes will rest on the Vindhyan range which stretches right across India, and separates the plains of Aryāvartta from the plateau of Dakṣiṇāpatha. From our high perch the Vindhyas look low and humble; that is why our poetic forefathers wove the tale that Agastya crushed the pride of the Vindhyas and pushed them down till a large part of their height sank into the bosom of the earth. North of the Vindhyas the land generally slopes down to the Yamunā. It also slopes west from the Arāvalli hills down to the Bētwa. Broad, flat elevations, probably the debris of the Arāvallis, accumulated through many millenniums, form the chief characteristic of the landscape. Mālva, says Sir John Malcolm, may

---

[1] Ep. Ind. ii. p. 1891. (Keilhorn).

"be concisely described as a table-land, in general open and highly cultivated, varied with small conical hills and low ridges, watered by numerous rivers and small streams, and favoured with a rich productive soil, and a mild climate, conducive to the health of man and the liberal supply of his wants and luxuries." [1]

The rivers of Mālva have been described by Kālidāsa with his delightful, unfailing poetic touch. They were the Vētravatī (Bētwa) whose sweet waters were undulating as if her face frowned when the cloud thundered near her banks,[2] the Vananadī on whose banks there were many jasmine-gardens, where women whose ear-lotuses had faded owing to the trouble of wiping the sweat on their cheeks, were gathering flowers,[3] the Nirvindhyā whose girdle was a row of noisy birds, and which showed navel-like eddies caused by stumbling against rocks,[4] the (Kālā) Sindhu, whose scanty water is braid-like and is white on account of the withered leaves which fall from the trees growing on its banks,[5] the Siprā the breeze from which, sweet-smelling on account of its contact with the fragrance of blown lotuses, lengthens the loud cooing of cranes,[6] the Gambhīrā whose limpid waters are like the pure mind[7] and the Carmaṇāvatī (Cambal), flowing with the blood of the kine offered by Rantidēva in the numerous sacrifices he performed, and appearing to the celestials like the earth's single-stringed pearl necklace.[8]

These rivers and many rivulets have cut their way through the basaltic rock of the Mālva plateau and made an intricate network of interlacing ravines. The rains washing down the trap-rock which

[1] Mal. Cen. Ind. i. pp. 3–4.

[2] Mēgh. 24.

[3] *Ib.* 26.

[4] *Ib.* 28.

[5] Mēgh. 29.

[6] *Ib.* 31.

[7] *Ib.* 42.

[8] *Ib.* 47, 48.

once covered the region and the vegetation that then clothed it have covered the greater part of Mālva with the black cotton soil called *mār* or *kāli* by the natives. Hence the country is highly fertile. The people are skilful and industrious cultivators. The principal crops are wheat, gram, *jowār*, cotton and poppy.[1]

From Kālidāsa's lovely poem, the *Meghadūta,* in which a yakṣa of Rāmagiri in the Central Provinces sends his message of love through a cloud-messenger to his wife who resided in the land of Kubēra in the Himālaya region, we learn that the garden-hedges of Mālva were whitened by *Kētaki* flowers open at the apex, its trees were disturbed by the village-birds building nests therein, the skirts of its *Jambu* forests were dark with ripe fruit, and the swans on their march north halted there for a few days.[2]

The *Āīn-i-Akbarī* says that in Mālva

> "at every two or three *Kos* clear and limpid streams are met on whose banks the willow grows wild, and the hyacinth and fragrant flowers of many hues, amid the abundant shade of trees. Lakes and green meads are frequent and stately palaces and fair country-homes breathe tales of fairy land. The climate is so temperate that in winter there is little need of warm clothing nor in summer of the cooling properties of saltpetre. The elevation of this province is somewhat above that of other areas of the country and every part of it is cultivable. Both harvests are excellent and especially wheat, poppy, sugarcane, mangoes, melons and grapes. In Hasilpur the vine bears twice in the year and betel-leaves of the finest quality. Cloth of the best texture is woven." [3]

---

1 Imp. Gaz. Ind. xvii. p. 100.

2 Mēgh. 23.

3 Tr. Jarret. ii. pp. 196–7.

In another passage the *Āīn-i-Akbarī* specially mentions the sweet mangoes and the luscious grapes and the *Kiauḍa* (*Kētaki, tāḻai*) of lasting perfume produced in Mālva as being specially famous.

In the parts of the country not brought under cultivation, there are dense forests, relics of the ancient Daṇḍakāraṇya, which abound in fine timber, especially the teak. The jungle is the abode of wild animals, such as the tiger, the leopard, the bear, the wolf, the hyaena, the wild hog, the antelope, the *nīlgāi* and the *sāmbur*. So there is no lack of game to tempt the bowman-hunter, king or forester. Among domestic animals, the horned cattle of Mālva have been so esteemed as to constitute a large article of export; but not so sheep and goats. Horses, too, have been reared but not of the quality raised in the neighbouring province of Kāthiāvāḍ. Camels have seldom been bred in Mālva, as it lacks the sandy and warm tracts such as are found in Mārvāḍ.

CHAPTER II

EARLY HISTORY OF MĀLVA

In very old times portions of the forest were cleared and towns built here and there in this region. The earliest of these towns was built by Mucukunda, son of Māndhātā, the first *Cakravartī*, or supreme lord of all India, who lived probably five thousand years ago. It was called Māhiṣmatī, after Mahiṣmān, a Haihaya King who ruled a century later. It was situated on the rocky bank of the Narmadā, at the foot of both the Vindhya and the Ṛkṣa (Sātpura) ranges, at a place where the two ranges approach each other. It is now called Māndhātā, the Ōmkāra Kṣētra, one of the holiest spots of India, on an island in the middle of the river. Māhiṣmatī was the capital of Arjuna Kārttavīrya, who was a great emperor and earned the title of Sahasrabāhu, the thousand-armed, because he was a doughty warrior. In the fort of Māhiṣmatī he confined a Rāvaṇa, who belonged to an age much earlier than that of the Rāvaṇa of the Rāmāyaṇa and had dared to challenge his might and invaded his dominions.

After Arjuna's death, his son, Jayadhvaja, reigned in Avanti, capital[1] of the province of Avanti, as Mālva was called in those days. About a thousand years later, the Bhōjas, a branch of the Yādavas, ruled in this part of the country. Avanti sank into obscurity till the age of Gautama Buddha when it became the great rival of Magadha and its king was the fierce Pradyōta (Pajjōta) who ruled at Ujjayinī and was the father of Vāsavadattā, beloved of Udayana, the king of the Vatsas. The story of

---

1 Pargiter. Ancient Ind. Hist. Trad. p. 366.

Udayana and Vāsavadattā became the subject of a beautiful drama by one of the earliest Sanskrit playwrights, Bhāsa, who lived a few centuries after and was also narrated in the *Bṛhatkathā* by Guṇāḍhya half a millennium and more after the time of the hero and the heroine and another half-millennium later, when Kālidāsa flourished, the story of Udayana was the subject of conversation among the old villagers of Avanti[1] who pointed out,

> "Here Vatsa-raja carried off the beloved daughter of Pradyōta; here too there was the golden garden of *tāla* belonging to that very king; here indeed roamed the elephant *Nalagiri* (a furious elephant given, according to legend, to Pradyōta by Indra) uprooting his post in madness: with these stories well-informed persons divert their relatives who come on a visit to this place."[2]

Pradyōta's eldest son, Gōpāla, gave up the throne to his brother Pālakka, and lived with his dear sister Vāsavadattā, at Kausāmbī, the Vatsa capital. Pālakka thereupon imprisoned Āryaka (Ajjaka), son of Gōpāla; but Śarvalaka, a Brāhmaṇa, managed to raise a rebellion in which Āryaka slew Pālakka and 'saved his family and name' as narrated in that most humorous drama, the *Mṛcchakaṭika* by King Śūdraka. This play, though a few centuries later than the events it deals with, gives us a vivid picture of life in Ujjayinī in old days. Rogue elephants sometimes broke loose, snapping the iron chain by means of which they were tethered and wandered with the broken chain dangling at the foot, while frightened women ran away so rapidly that their anklets dropped down, till the elephants which looked like great mountains were felled down with an iron pole.

---

[1] Mēgh. 30.

[2] *Ib.* 32. (Pathak).

In the streets abounded Bauddha monks each carrying a staff, a water-jar and a begging-bowl. Dogs were sound asleep in the shops that looked out on the market. Hetairae abounded, some who led as self-respecting lives as the chastest of wives. The science and art of thieving were cultivated by the *proteges* of Skanda; they made holes in the walls where the bricks had been eaten away by nitre and broke into houses. The house of rich people had a number of courtyards and the gateways of each were decorated on festival occasions; there were rows of balconies in the first court brilliant as the moon or as sea-shells, In the second court cart-bullocks, buffaloes, horses, monkeys and elephants were kept. In the third court was a gaming-table. The fourth court was reserved for musical performances, generally by courtezans. The kitchen was in the fifth court. Goldsmiths were working in the sixth court making jewels for the ladies of the household and there perfumes were being ground. Doves and parrots and other pet-birds were kept in the seventh court. The inmates lived in the eighth court where there was an orchard. The king owned a garden outside the city; therein could be seen 'trees adorned with fruits and flowers, clinging creepers interlacing round' their trunks. Monkeys were hanging from the 'leafy tree-top.' The administration of the city was so much advanced that it possessed a law-court presided over by a judge and provided with beadles, gild-wardens and clerks. The procedure of trials was fixed by laws, though even in those days the rich man could bend the law to suit his own purposes.

The merry life of the people of Ujjayinī is also described by Kālidāsa. Śūdraka and Kālidāsa lived much later than the age we are dealing with. But as social life in India changes so slowly that social conditions and the manner of life of the people depicted in the mantras of the Ṛg Vēda and the Atharva Vēda exist almost without change to-day in villages, it is quite probable that the Ujjayinī of Śūdraka and Kālidāsa was in every respect the same as that of Pālakka. Says Kālidāsa,

> "In the balconies of the palaces of Ujjayinī from the eyes of the townswomen "shot" unsteady side-glances dazzled by flashes of lightning." "Exposed for sale in the markets were brilliant pearlstrings with a precious stone in the centre, crores of conch-shells and pearl-oysters, emeralds dark-green like young grass, sending forth rays of light. Ladies perfumed their hair with incense which escaped from the lattice-windows. In the palaces filled with the ..ent of flowers and marked with red lac from the feet of fair women, danced tame peacocks."[1]

Into such a lovely city spread in the 4th century B. C. the mild asceticism propounded by Gautama Buddha and it soon became popular. Bauddha Sanyāsīs found the summits of the hills of Mālva and their peaceful atmosphere conducive to their studies and yoga practices; they founded several monasteries there. Bauddha monasteries generally contained a very much larger number of *Bhikkhus* than Brāhmaṇa or Jaina ones, because the rules of the Saugata order were much laxer than those of the other congregations of Sanyāsīs. Hence the *Sanghārāmās* of the followers of Gautama were built at spots which were sufficiently remote from towns to permit of peaceful meditation and doctrinal debates, but yet close enough to the capitals of kings or local chiefs to enable them to get a plentiful supply of gifts of provisions for their larder and to attract crowds of men and women to help to celebrate their gay festivals. The most populous of

[1] Mēgh. 27, 33, 34.

their monasteries in Mālva was that of Sāñci, a village which rests on a hill, less than 300 ft. in height.

> "As with all the neighbouring offshoots of the Vindhyas, its formation is of sandstone, which slopes, layer on layer, in shelving masses down its sides wherein the Buddhist builders of old found a quarry for their stone ready to hand and easily worked. In the various hues of this stone and in its rugged crags there is a wonderful charm alike of form and colour, and this charm is enhanced by the wealth of jungle shrubs and trees which spring from every nook and crevice among the giant boulders. The vegetation grows free and dense on all the steeper slopes around the hill, but most luxuriantly on its southern half, in places where the high and shady cliffs afford shelter against the sun. Here the evergreen *Khirni* tree, with its sombre foliage, is especially abundant, and here in the early spring the *dhāk* or 'flame of the forest', as it has been so happily called, sets the hill-side ablaze with its clusters of gorgeous blossoms, affording a strangely gay and dazzling setting to the grey ruins that crest the ridges above." [1]

In a few centuries after the death of Gautama, Eastern Mālva (Ākara) became separate from Western Mālva (Avanti) and the whole province came to be called Akarāvanti. Aśōka ruled over it as *Yuvarāja* before he ascended the throne of Magadha. Vidiśa (now Bhilsa), 120 miles east of Ujjayinī, was its chief town. Aśōka, to signify his reverence for the great ascetic Gautama, whose personality dominated the minds of many Indians for about five centuries after his Nirvāṇa, built at Sāñci, or Kākanāda, as it was called, in inscriptions, a *stūpa* of brick, (each brick measuring 16″ × 10″ × 3″), probably "roughly hemispherical in shape, with a raised terrace encompassing its base and a railing and a stone umbrella crowning its summit." [2] Aśōka also set up a pillar on which was inscribed the *dhamma* that he preached for the benefit of laymen.

---

[1] Marsh. Guide to Sāñci, p. 3.

[2] Marsh. *op. cit.* p. 32.

About half a century after the death of Aśōka, Kings of the Sāmavedīya Brāhmaṇa family of the Suṅgas succeeded to the rule of North India. Their main capital was Vidiśa. Pusyamitra, the first Śuṅga King, has been falsely accused of persecuting the Bauddhas, on the strength of an idle legend recorded in late times. As a matter of fact, under his rule and that of his immediate successors, the brick *stūpa* of Sāñci was furnished with a stone envelope which made the diameter of the *stūpa* increase to over 120 feet and its height to about 54 feet, and a terrace was then added to it.

> "Over the masonry courses of both dome and terrace was laid a thick coat of concrete, finished off, no doubt, with finer plaster, and possibly embellished with swags or garlands in relief and hanging from projecting turns, and further relieved with colours and gilding."[1]

On the top was then put an umbrella supported by a pedestal box containing relics of the Buddha with a railing round it. The next addition was a ground balustrade of stone, given by various people and made in imitation of a wooden railing. Then in still later times were put up a processional path, a stairway flanked by balustrades and encompassing the terrace, gateways (*tōraṇa*) in the four directions, etc.

The last king of the Śuṅga line to rule at Vidiśa was Bhagabhadra, and in the fourteenth year of his reign, Heliodoros, a Yavana (Greek), ambassador of Antialkidas, Yavana King of Takṣaśilā, built a stone pillar with the figure of Garuḍa on its top. This pillar is now standing at a place called Besnagar, near Bhopal, and was probably placed in the front of a Viṣṇu temple of wood which has now completely vanished. Heliodoros calls himself a Bhāgavata,

[1] Marsh. *op. cit.* p. 33.

which word, along with its synonyms, Sāttvata and Pāñcarātra, meant in those days a worshipper of Viṣṇu, a Vaiṣṇava; apparently in the pre-Christian centuries the walls of caste were not rigid and it was not impossible for a *mlēccha* (foreigner) to become a Vaiṣṇava. This pillar is also noteworthy because it proves that schools of the Vaiṣṇava Agamas had made notable advances in philosophic and ethical thought long before the IInd Century B. C. They took over the simple concept of the three steps of Viṣṇu, representing in early Vedic times the three positions of the Sun—at sunrise, noon, and sunset—and allegorized them as the three steps in the path that leads to immortality (*trīṇi amuta-padāni*) viz.,

> "self-control, self-denial, and watchfulness" (*damo cāgo apramāda*) for we find inscribed on the Garuḍa pillar *Triṇi amutapadini*. . . . (*pta*) *anuthitāni, nayamti svaga* (*m*) *damo cago apramādo*, 'three are the steps to immortality which. . . followed lead to heaven, (namely) self-control, self-denial, and watchfulness." [1]

The worship of Viṣṇu and of Śiva as prescribed in the *Agamas*, giving ample room for the manifestation of the devotional (*bhakti*) instincts of man and associated with a severe moral and spiritual training were formidable rivals of the Jaina and Bauddha cults from their inception; as these latter made little provision for man's natural instincts of devotion to God, they soon obscured the former and superseded entirely the latter, so that it does not exist any more in the land of its birth and prevails only in foreign countries shorn of the Indian associations which are its soul and body.

A century or two later, another city rose to importance in this region; it was called Daśapura, probably

[1] A. S. R. 1908–09. p. 125.

because it was made up of ten villages, which together formed a unit of local administration. It was later called Mandasor and is to-day the headquarters of the district of the same name in Central India. It is situated on the banks of the Siwana, a branch of the Siprā.

About this time or perhaps a little earlier, Avanti became the headquarters of a line of Pontiffs of the Jainas. Then Avanti became subject to Saka-Pallava Rājās, who came over the sea from Śakastāna on the borders of Persia. They were defeated and driven out of Mālva in tho year 56 B. C. by a great hero whose personal name is unknown, but who had the titles of *Vikramāditya* and *Śakāri*; from this date began the *Vikrama Samvatsara*, the era used in Northern India up to our own days. After his time Jaina teachers began again to abound in Mālva, and to-day the remains of numerous Jaina temples can be seen in this province. In 77 A.D. Castana, the Śaka, was crowned king of Mālva and Surāṣṭra. From the coronation of this Śaka king began the era, now called the *Śālivāhana Śaka era*, which prevails throughout Southern India. These Śaka Rājās, who were called also Kṣatrapas or Mahākṣatrapas, ruled till 398 A.D. and during their rule, the trade of India with Europe was much developed and the old town of Ujjayinī became the *entrepot* of India's foreign commerce. Goods from the North, the East and the South were gathered in that city by Śrēṣṭhīs (Seṭṭis) whose descendants are the Seths of modern days, and sent to the seaports on the western coasts and thence to Egypt and Europe. Greek astrologico-astronomical knowledge spread from Alexandria to Ujjayinī and this, blended with Vedic astronomy, gave birth to modern Indian astronomy, at first cultivated by the scholars of Ujjayinī which hence became the central longitude from which all astronomical calculations were made.

In the third century the power of the Śaka Kṣatrapas declined chiefly on account of the rise of Nāgas, Muruṇḍas, Abhiras and other tribes. At the end of the IIIrd century A. D. a new line of kings whose names ended in Varmā began to rule in Eastern Mālva. The famous Candravarmā, one of the early kings of this line, built the famous Iron Pillar set up now at Mehrauli in Delhi.

The last of the Śaka kings of Mālva was killed by Candragupta, son of Samudragupta, disguised as a woman. With the extinction of the Śaka dynasty, Mālva became more or less subordinate to the Guptas. Mandasor (then called Daśapura), mentioned in the inscriptions of the early years of the Christian era, rose to prominence under Kumāragupta's rule.

In the VIth century the Hūṇas captured Mālva. Toramāṇa Śāha and his son, Mihiragula, both devotees of Śiva, became its rulers. Then arose a great Brāhmaṇa hero, called Viṣṇuvarddhana Yaśōdharmadēva, who, as he tells us in his Pillar Inscription found near Daśapura, broke the power of the Hūṇas and ruled as the over-lord of the whole country from

> "the neighbourhood of Lauhitya (Brahmaputra) to the mountain of Mahēndra (in Orissa), the lands at the foot of which are impenetrable because of the groves of palmyra trees, and from the Mountain of snow (the Himālaya), the table-lands of which are embraced by the Gaṅgā, to the Western Ocean." [1]

Many great poets and scientific men flourished in Mālva during the reign of Yaśōdharma Dēva, who was also hailed as *Vikramāditya Sakāri*. There is

[1] Gupta Insc., p. 148.

a tradition that "nine gems" (*navaratnāni*) were the ornaments of the Court of *Navavikrama*; at the head of them was Kālidāsa, the greatest poet of India and a native of Mālva; hence some scholars regard him as belonging to the VIth century. Others of the "nine gems" were Varāha Mihira, (who himself informs us that he belonged to the VIth century), the author of the first extensive and systematic treatises on Indian astronomy and astrology, Amarasiṁha, the lexicographer, Dhanvantari, a medical writer, Bhaṭṭi, Vararuci, Śaṅku, Ghaṭakarpara, and Kṣapaṇaka, poets.

Yaśōdharmadēva's immediate descendants continued the patronage of literary men, but their power soon waned; the province of Mālva broke up into the "Seven Mālvas" and became the constant battleground between the Pratihāras of Kanauj (Kānyakubja) and the Rāṣṭrakūṭas of Mālkhēḍ (Mānyakhēṭa), who shared between themselves the allegiance of its princelets. But the political troubles of Mālva did not interrupt the steady pursuit of Saṁskṛta studies; not only did Vedic lore flourish, but a steady stream of Bauddha scholars flowed to China, and in this period Buddharakṣita, Guṇabhadra, Paramārtha and Atigupta, among others, went from Mālva to China and made translations of Bauddha Saṁskṛta works for the benefit of the Chinese.

CHAPTER III

THE PARAMĀRAS

The (*Navasāhasāṅkacarita* by Padmagupta, one of the greatest poets of Dhārā, gives the legendary history of the rise of the Paramāras, better than the inscriptions which contain *praśastis*, eulogies, of these kings. It says,

"There (on mount Arbuda) the wise house-priest (Vasiṣṭha) of the Ikṣvākus made a sage's grove, rich in wild rice, fruits, roots, fire-wood and *Kuśa*-grass.

His wish-granting cow was once stolen and carried away by the son of Gādhi (Viśvāmitra), as was that of Jamadagni by Arjuna, Kṛtavīrya's offspring.

Arundhatī, upon whose bosom the silk garment was bathed with tears, became a log, on account of her husband's wrath.

Thereupon the first of the judges of the Atharvaṇa songs (Vasiṣṭha), with holy sayings, threw an offering into the fire, which, kindling up with broad flames, seemed to bear an ascetic's hair braid.

Quickly a man sprang out of the fire, with bow and crown and golden armour.

By him the cow of the wise man, led away by Viśvāmitra, was brought back, as the sun brings back the light of day, which has been led away by the thick darkness.

Then the grove-maidens took the cheek, wet with tears of joy, from the supporting hand which is worshipped by the devout.

He received from the sage the fitting name of Paramāra—killer of the enemy—and a ruler's power over the globe, before whom all the parasols of all other kings were shut." [1]

In the post-Christian centuries when new families rose to power and acquired the rule of large districts,

---

[1] Ind. Ant. xxxvi, p. 162, (Nav. Sāh. Car. xi; 64-71.)

it was the fashion to invest them with Kṣattriya status and invent an eponymous ancestor for them, connecting him with Vedic Ṛṣis or epic heroes. Such eponymous heroes were Pallava, Cālukya and Paramāra. Princes who claimed descent from Paramāra possessed the fort of Acalagaḍh near Mount Ābū and ruled over the surrounding districts with Candrāvatī as capital. In the IX century a line of Paramāra princes became famous as the lords of Mālva and rose to such heights of power that they became the protectors of the original Paramāras of Acalagaḍh. This new dynasty was founded by Upēndra, also called Kṛṣṇarāja. Like all founders of new dynasties he had to contend with neighbouring princes, and he celebrated his victories and established the status of supreme sovereignty by enlisting the aid of learned Brāhmaṇas and performing many Vedic sacrifices. Says Padmagupta,

> "this sacrificer, before whom Indra was afraid (lest by performing 100 *Yajñas*, Upēndra should usurp Indra's throne), whose body was rendered holy by (many *avabhṛta*) baths i.e. those taken at the end of sacrifices, decked the earth with golden *yūpas*."[1]

Therefore an inscription describes him as

> "Upēndrarāja, whose fame was proclaimed by the immortals, satisfied by the multitude of all sacrifices,—who was a jewel among the twice-born and gained high honour of kinghood by his valour."[2]

He lived soon after 800 A. D. His son was also a great warrior,

> "a lion for the elephant-like hostile kings, the best of heroes, Srī Vairisiṁha, who composed his own eulogy by (erecting) pillars of victory (everywhere) on the earth that is bounded by the four oceans."[2]

---

[1] Nav. xi. 78.

[2] E. I. i. 237.

The building of *Jayasthambhas* was an old Indian custom which Vairisiṁha followed.

> "From him sprang Śrī Sīyaka, a prince (standing) in the first rank of conquerors, whose foot-stool was resplendent and coloured by the rays of the jewels in the diadems of kings.—he, the crowd of whose enemies was submerged in the waves of the waters of the blade in his hand." [1]

From the praises accorded to these Paramāra kings of the IX century, it can be deduced, that each of them had to struggle hard with neighbouring princes and by means of victories over them build on firm foundations the rising power of Mālva.

> "From him sprang Śrī Vākpati, a sun for (those) water-lilies the eyes of the maidens of Avanti, (he who was) resplendent with the rays of the sword in his hand, who resembled Śatamakha (Indra) and whose armies drank the waters of the Gaṅgā and of the Ocean." [1]

This is the first definite reference to Ujjayinī as the capital of the Paramāras. A legend is narrated of him that while encamped at Daśapura,

> "during his father's life-time he found the people of that district on the verge of rebellion. He called the leaders together and by his persuasive words calmed their apprehensions and averted a revolt. From that day he was given the *biruda* of Vākpati or the lord of eloquence. The bards also credit him with a campaign in Kāmarūpa (Assam) in which he was successful after 27 days' fighting." [2]

This explains the phrase in the inscription that his armies drank the waters of the Gaṅgā and the Ocean.

The inscription goes on to say that

> "from him was born Vairisiṁha II, whom the people call Vajraṭa Svāmi; by that king famous Dhārā was indicated, when he slew the crowd of his enemies with the sharp edge (*dhārā*) of his sword."

---

[1] E. I. i. 237.

[2] Dhar State Gaz. p. 130.

The rising strength of the Paramāras roused the jealousy of rival princes and the necessity arose for changing the capital from Ujjayinī to Dhārā which was better fitted naturally for effective fortification. To distinguish the name of the place from dhārā (sword-edge) it was called Dhārānagari, but yet the temptation to play on the several meanings of the word (dhārā) could not be resisted by later poets, as will be noticed later on. Padmagupta says of Vairisiṁha that he was a

> "lion to his enemies; his fame, bright as jasmine and like the moon, was as a mane to him; when the kingly swans saw the bow of this prince, who was like Paulomi's husband, they forsook the land, as the regal swans forsook the pond when they saw Indra's pond."[1]

From him

> "sprang he who is called his glorious majesty Harṣa, the sound of whose trumpets was beautiful like the noise of the roaring of mighty elephants in the armies of numerous hostile kings, he, who, equalling the snake-eater (Garuḍa) in fierceness, took in battle the wealth of King Khoṭṭiga."[2]

The Garuḍa was figured on the flags of Paramāras, who were mostly worshippers of Viṣṇu. Khoṭṭiga who was defeated by this King, called by the several names, Harṣa Śiṁha, Harak Singh, Śrī-Harṣadēva, Śīyaka II, was the Rāṣṭrakūṭa king of Mānyakhēṭa, who died in 972 A. D. A Prākṛta poet, Dhanapāla, says in his *Pāiyalacchi* that he composed that work

> "when one thousand years of the Vikrama era and twenty-nine besides had passed, when Maṇṇakhēḍa (Mānyakhēṭa) had been plundered in consequence of an attack (made) by the lord of Mālva."[3]

---

1 Nav. xi. 83-4 (I.A. xxxvi. pp. 163-4).

2 E. I. i. p. 237.

3 E. I. ii. p. 192.

Śīyaka II also conquered the lord of Rāḍūpāṭī, besides the head of a Kṣattriya house of the Hūna clan.[1] He was the first of a brilliant series of hero-Kings of Mālva under whom that province became the leading one in India. Śīyaka II was succeeded by Utpalarāja, otherwise called Muñja, and Vākpatirāja II. He was a great warrior, a poet and a patron of poets.[2]

Muñja was

> "the sole abode of good qualities, adorned the whole earth, the growth of whose riches was proportionate to the deposits of wealth (which he received) from foes that were conquered by his bravery, who, cultivating eloquence, high poetry and the art of reasoning, completely mastered the lore of the *Śāstras*, who is ever praised by the virtuous as his glorious majesty, Vākpati; he whose lotus-feet were coloured by the jewels on the heads of the Karnāṭas, Lāṭas, Kēralas and Cōlas and who possessed the fame of a tree of paradise, since he granted to a crowd of suppliants whatever they desired; who conquering Yuvarāja and slaying his generals, as victor, raised on high his sword in Tripurī."[3]

In this eulogy the mention of the Cōlas is merely formal, because Muñja never came in contact with them; nor can be recovered any details about his fights with the Lāṭas or people of South Gujarāt, which had just been seized by a Caulukya prince named Bārappa, probably some connection of Mūlarāja, the founder of the Caulukya (Solaṅki) dynasty of Gujarāt. Yuvarāja was the second Kalacuri king of that name, who ruled over the Cēdi country with Tripurī (near Jabalpur) as his capital. He

> "purified the town of Tripurī so that it was like Indra's city,"[4]

but was conquered by Muñja who slew him and his generals and captured Tripurī[5] Muñja's most power-

---

[1] Nav. Sāh. Car. xi. p. 89-90. [2] E. I. i. pp. 224-27.
[3] E. I. i. p. 237. [4] E. I. xii. p. 215. [5] E. I. i. p. 237.

ful foe was Tailapa II, Raṇaraṅgabhīma, terrible on the field of battle, the exterminator of the Rāṣṭrakūṭa empire and founder of that of the second line of Western Cālukyas. Six times (a legend makes it sixteen) did Muñja invade the Cālukya territory and defeat Tailapa; he then added to his titles those of the Rāṣṭrakūṭa emperors, viz., Amōghavarṣa, Srī Vallabha, Pṛthvīvallabha. But a rapidly moving column of Tailapa's soldiers kept on harassing, whenever possible, Muñja's subjects and the King of Dhārā resolved to crush Tailapa finally. Rudrāditya, Muñja's minister, was ill but yet tried very hard to dissuade the King from starting on this project. He reminded Muñja of an old prediction to the effect that destruction would overtake him if he should cross the Gōdāvarī. But Muñja looked upon Tailapa with contempt, for he had defeated the Cālukya six times before. In his overweening confidence, he crossed the Gōdāvarī and pitched his camp south of that river. Rudrāditya heard of the King's headstrong conduct and in despair entered the flames of a funeral pile. Tailapa, with a strong army, whose ranks were swollen with contingents, sent by several of his feudatories, suddenly fell upon Muñja's army and cut it to pieces.

In this battle took part, among others, Bhillama II, a *Mahāsāmanta*, 'feudatory governor' belonging to the Yādava clan, which claimed descent from Śrī Kṛṣṇa, who therefore bore the hereditary title of "Supreme lord of the town of Dvāravatī" (Dvārakā) and was a vassal of Tailapa's. He took Muñja prisoner, binding him with a rope of *muñja* grass, and thus 'rendered firm the sovereign authority of Raṇaraṅgabhīma.' Muñja was put in prison and confined in a wooden cage and on his head was heaped insult on insult. While he was under confinement, Mṛṇāḷavatī, widowed sister of Tailapa fell in love with him and attended to his wants.

Meanwhile, certain of Muñja's ministers dug a tunnel which led to his prison in order that he might escape through it. One morning when Muñja was standing before a mirror, Mṛṇāḷavatī approached him from behind and saw reflected in the mirror, her own wrinkled face by the side of the handsome face of her lover. Her face turned dark with the thought that his love for her would die soon. Muñja easily read the idea that was passing through her mind and said to her,—

> "Says Muñja, O weep not, Mṛṇāḷavatī, for thy fairness departed,
>
> One pounds the hard crystals of sugar, the powder still tastes quite delicious."

But his face remained clouded, as he was brooding over the plans of escape. Mṛṇāḷavatī, to make sure of the state of his mind, first gave him saltless food to eat and then food with too much salt; he swallowed both without noticing the difference. Then in order to wheedle his secret out of him, she questioned him in a charming voice, and at last he said to her,—

> "I am about to escape from this prison by means of a tunnel; if you will come with me, I will make you my chief queen."

She thought that his love for an elderly widow, who had no good looks to stimulate love, would die soon, but answered,—

> "Wait a minute, I will fetch my casket of jewels,"

and then rushed to her brother and betrayed to him her lover's secret plans. Muñja was thereupon bound with cords and led like a chained monkey to beg from door to door, moaning,—

> "The hearts of men are filled with grief when they confide in women,
> Who utter charming words of love to captivate all minds."

He lamented,—

> "My horses, chariots, elephants, my footmen, servants, all are gone;
> O Rudrāditya, now in heaven, call me; to join thee I crave."

Muñja was finally led to the place of execution, and he was told to think of his favourite deity (*iṣṭadēva*). He, then, in imitation of the well-known Vedic mantra recited during obsequies, ordering each element of the body to go to the God whence it came, exclaimed,—

> "Fortune, his wife, will go to Gōvinda;
> To heroes' heaven will go heroic fame;
> When Muñja has departed from this earth,
> Sarasvatī, abode of fame will be
> Without a column to support her seat."

He was then executed and his head was fixed on a stake planted in the courtyard of the palace of Tailapa II, and bathed everyday with sour buttermilk. Verily, the Karṇāṭa King had forgotten the old Indian ideals of *Dharmayuddha*, warfare guided by ethical considerations, which inculcated chivalry to fallen foes, which required the victorious king to grant respite to the defeated one for the purpose of collecting a fresh army, which forbade the victor to take advantage of the difficulties of the enemy in the field of battle and which ordained that all hatred should cease with the cessation of hostilities!

When young Bhōja, nephew of Muñja, heard of the savage treatment accorded to his uncle, he vowed that he would avenge the insult when he became King. Poets composed elegies on the misfortunes of Muñja. One pitiful lament may be quoted :—

"That treasure of glory, that Muñja, the lord of Avanti and elephants,
That long since was born as abode of Sarasvatī, Goddess of Fortune,
The lord of Karṇāṭa imprisoned, despite of the wisdom of ministers,
Impaled on a sharp stake; O verily dark is the path of one's Karma.
The Lord of Ayōdhyā, he died out of sorrow for parting with Rāma,
His carcase preserved in an oil-cask, delayed were his funeral rites long
Beyond the due season, prescribed for the purpose by ordinances of Rsis.
Bewildered with *mōha* of riches, thou laugh'st when disaster o'ertakes one.
Thou feelest it strange that the fortunes of men are inconstant? Yet knowest,
In watering fields with the water-wheel, the bucket now empty is full soon;
The bucket that's full is soon found to contain not a drop of water."

Another elegy ran,

"He's decked with a death's head, and his follower Bhṛṅgī is shrivelled in body;
His riches an old bull; the state of the Great God is deplorable truly!
Then tell me, O sage, how poor wretches will fare when misfortune and misery
Shall reach us and stand on our heads which are weary with load of disaster!
The wide sea for moat and great Lankā for fortress, when fortune deserted him,
Great Rāvaṇa lost all. O Muñja, what room for despair in thy case is?"

Muñja was an accomplished poet and attracted to his court a large number of scholars and poets whom he liberally rewarded. Many of Muñja's verses are found scattered in Merutuṅga's *Prabandha cintāmaṇi*, Ballāla's *Bhojaprabandha* and similar chronicles and also in works on *Alaṅkāra* composed in later times. Padmagupta, the greatest of the poets of his court, thus eulogized him.

> "We worship his Majesty Vākpati, only support of the creeper of heaven, great Vāṇī.
> Through favour of Muñja we walk on the path of this prince of all poets on earth in our life-time."

Others of his *proteges* were Dhanañjaya, author of the treatise on dramatic composition, *Daśarūpa*, his brother Dhanika, who wrote a commentary thereon, called *Daśarūpāvalōka* and another work called *Kāvya nirṇaya* and who calls himself the *Mahāsādhyapālā*, of Utpalarāja, Dhanapāla, author of the Lexicon, *Pāiyalacchi*, and Halāyudha, who composed a *varttika* on the *Piṅgala sūtras*, who praises Vākpati "as the tree of paradise that grants the wishes of all suppliants."

Notwithstanding his constant wars, and his ardent devotion to the muses, Muñja found time for architectural activities. He is

> "credited with considerable activity in the erection of buildings and the biggest of the twelve artificial lakes round Dhārā, called the Muñja-sāgara, is said to have been one of his undertakings. Tradition has it that numerous fine bathing-ghats surrounded it, but of these there are now no traces, and if they existed they must have been silted up. The tank near Jahāz mahāl at Māṇḍu known as the Muñja talāo is also supposed to be his handiwork. Ghats are said to have been erected by him at Māndhātā, Mahēśvar, and Kubja-saṅgam (near Dharmapurī) and he is credited with improving the fortifications of Ujjayinī and beautifying Dhār with many buildings." [1]

[1] Dhar State Gaz., p. 135.

These were not the only forms of generosity which Vākpati II practised. He built and repaired temples and gave grants of lands to them as well as to learned Brāhmaṇa teachers. Thus he made in 980 A.D. to the Bhaṭṭarikā Bhaṭṭēśvarī, the form of Kālī who was worshipped as the presiding deity of Ujjayinī, a grant of the village of Sembalapuraka. When he made the grant the king was at Bhāgavatapura, and the purpose of the gift was to provide for the worship of the goddess in the temple, and keeping the building in repair.[1] A specimen of the second kind of gift was the grant in 974 A.D. made while he was staying at Ujjayinī of the village of Pīpparīkā on the north banks of the Narmadā, to the very learned Brāhmaṇa teacher, Śrī Vasantācārya who had migrated from Ahicchatra south to Mālva.[2]

Sindhurāja (Sindhula) was Muñja's younger brother. He took to wife a Nāga princes, named Śaśiprabhā, the daughter of Vajrāṅkuśa of Ratnāvati. The relations between Muñja and Sindhula were not always pleasant.[3] It is said that on account of Sindhula's unruly behaviour, he was banished once. He then settled in Gujarāt near the town of Kāśahrada near the modern Ahmadābād; ultimately he made peace with Muñja, who, when he started on his last expedition against Tailapa, "placed the earth in Sindhurāja's arms." After Muñja's death he mounted the throne and made Padmagupta his chief court-poet. The poet refers to this when he says :—

> "When his Majesty Vākpati was about to ascend to heaven, he placed a seal on my songs; Sindhurāja, the younger brother of that brother of poets, now breaks it."[4]

---

[1] Ind. Ant. xiv. p. 159.

[2] *Ib.* vi. p. 53.

[3] E. I. i. pp. 228–29.

[4] Nav. Car. i. 7.

Sindhurāja succeeded his brother in 997 A.D. He assumed the *birudas* of *Navasāhasāṅka* and *Kumāra Nārāyaṇa*. His chief minister was Yaśobhaṭa Rāmāṅgada and chief court-poet and biographer, Padmagupta. It was fashionable in those days for each king, as soon as he was crowned, to set about fighting with his royal neighbours. Sindhurāja fought with and defeated the chief of the Hūṇa Kṣattriya house as well as the rulers of the Kōsalas, of the inhabitants of Vāgaḍa, of the Lāṭas and the Muralas. The Kōsalas were the people of Mahākōsalā, south of the Vindhyas, in the Central Provinces. Vāgaḍa was close to the north-western frontier of Mālva. The Muralas were the feudatories of the Caulukyas in the west coast of India.

From the Prabandhakāras (authors of the chronicles dealing with mediaeval Rājās) we also hear of Sindhurāja's struggles with the Caulukyas, Cāmuṇḍarāja and Vallabharāja of Aṇahilvāḍ. Cāmuṇḍarāja was a man of evil life and finally abdicated in favour of his son, Vallabharāja and proceeded on a pilgrimage to Benares. On his way through Mālva, Cāmuṇḍarāja was deprived of his umbrella of state and other marks of royalty. He proceeded on his journey, but sent his son a message praying him to take revenge for this insult on the Mālva King.[1] Vallabharāja, also called Madanaśaṅkara invaded Mālva and invested the fortifications of Dhārā, but died of small-pox during the siege. Hence Bhōja, son of Sindhurāja, inherited another feud, this time with the Caulukya Rājās of Aṇahilvāḍ, capital of Gujarāt.

Sindurāja unlike his successor preferred to reside at Ujjayinī, for Padmagupta says,

"residing in the town of Ujjayinī, he rules all around."[2]

---

1 Dhar State Gaz. p. 140. Rāsmālā i. 76. I.A. xxxvi. p. 171.

2 Nav. xi. 99.

Bhōja was the son of Sindhurāja and nephew of Muñja. Like Kṣāttriya princes throughout the ages, he underwent an extensive course of studies. He acquired a ripe Saṁskṛta scholarship. He studied all the available Saṁskṛta books on king-craft. He became skilful in the use of the thirty-six weapons used in those days in warfare. He mastered the sixty-four arts which had then grown to perfection in India. Above all, he became an accomplished poet and a scholar who could hold his own in learned debates against the greatest scholars of his time. Three hundred years after his death a story of his youth found its way into books. It was probably not based on fact, but it is too interesting to be consigned to oblivion. Muñja, it would appear, became jealous of his nephew's popularity; but matters came to a head when a celebrated astrologer examined the horoscope of young Bhōja and proclaimed the following prediction :—

> "For fifty years and five and six more moons besides three days
> Shall Bhōja rule o'er Dakṣiṇāpatha and Gauḍa too,"

i. e., all over India, both north and south of the Vindhyas. 'Rule' in this prophetic utterance merely meant the premier place among Kings. Muñja thereupon resolved to remove this possible rival to his glory and ordered some men of the lowest caste, Gonds from the interior of Mālva, to take Bhōja to the heart of the forest and slay him there. The ruffians, however, were smitten with pity on beholding the beauty of his person and hearing the sweetness of his cultured voice. They agreed to take to the king a communication from Bhōja. Thereupon the young prince-poet wrote on the leaf of a tree a stanza to the following effect :—

> "Māndhātā, lord of earth, the ornament of the foremost age of all, is gone;
>
> Where's he who bridged the sea, the foe of Rāvaṇa, possessor of ten heads,
>
> Yudhiṣṭhira and more, many more, O king, have reigned for long before thy time;
>
> Along with none of them did go the earth, with thee alone 'twill pass away!"

Muñja shed bitter tears when he read this missive and ordered Bhōja to be brought back to him and restored to his rightful place in the royal court. The legend goes on to say that Muñja, for the purpose of expiating his sinful attempt at murder, performed a pilgrimage to the Dharmāraṇya lying on the east of the lesser Rann of Kacch and founded there a town called Muñjapuram.

On the death of Sindhurāja in the second decade of the XI century, Bhōja succeeded to the throne and permanently shifted the capital to Dhārā, which was situated on an island surrounded by a ring of lakes joined together by deep ditches, with ramparts 40 to 50 feet high rising above them. Hence he was frequently referred to as Dhārēśvara, a title not accorded to his predecessors.

CHAPTER IV

BHŌJA'S CONTEMPORARIES

Let us study awhile the political map of India in the first half of the XIth century and consider which dynasties ruled over the different provinces into which India was divided and which Kings were the contemporaries of the great Bhōja Rājā, the most accomplished of the Kings of the time. Gāndhāra was the border province in the North-west of India since Vedic times, if not earlier; but the Brāhmaṇa Sāhi kings of that district had, before the century began, been driven to the banks of the Sindhu. From the commencement of the century, when Sindhurāja was on the throne of Mālva and for several years after Bhōja succeeded him, Maḥmūd Yāmin al Daula, Amīr of Ghaznī, conducted almost every year his daring raids into Indian territory. In the words of the great Muhammadan *savant*, Al Bērūnī, he

> "utterly ruined the prosperity of the country and performed there wonderful exploits, by which the Hindus became like atoms of dust scattered in all directions, and like a tale of old in the mouths of the people."[1]

The Brāhmaṇa Sāhi Kings had to bear the brunt of the onslaught. Jayapāla sought to wipe off the disgrace of defeat by entering the burning flames. His son, Ānandapāla, fought valiantly with "Hammīra (the Amīr), leader of the Turuṣka army, full of stratagem" and, though helped by contingents sent by several Rājās, could not stem the flood of invasion. Ānandapāla's son, Trilōcanapāla was also defeated by Maḥmūd, and "the royal glory of the Sāhis vanished (down to their very) name."[2] The

[1] Ind. tr. Sachau, i. p. 22.

[2] Rājatar. vii. 66.

greater part of the Punjab was added to the dominions of the Ghaznavī dynasty. Sindh was conquered by Wazīr Abdur-Razzāq, the general of Maḥmūd in 1025 A.D. and passed to the hands of the Amīr of Ghaznī.

Kāśmīr, protected by her mountain-walls, escaped the cruel attentions of the Amīr of Ghaznī, and was enjoying the benefits of peace after the stormy reign of the dissolute Queen Didda, under the rule of the Lōhara Kings. Saṅgrāmarāja, the first of this line, helped Trilōcanapāla in his struggle with Maḥmūd. Anantavarmā, patron of scholars, succeeded him in 1028 A.D. and, when the Sāhis were finally expelled from their throne and their province was brought under Ghaznavī dominion, the relics of the house of Brāhmaṇa sovereigns, Rudrapāla and others, took service in the Kāśmīr court and were given large salaries to enable them to keep up their royal style of living. Petty Himalayan states, like that of Camba were beyond the reach of the long arm of Maḥmūd and were ruled by their own chiefs, feudatories of Kāśmīr. Śālavāhana and Somavarmā of Camba were Bhōja's contemporaries. They built shrines of timber adorned with graceful wood-carving.[1] But Maḥmūd cruelly plundered and destroyed the holy temples of Nāgarkōṭ and other places in the Kāngra Valley, and the ancient Trigarta, which Rajas of Jālandhara had to rebuild, when the flood of Islam ebbed from their boundaries. Indracandra of Kāngra built, after Maḥmūd's retreat, a Śiva temple with a *nandi* in front, covered by an open pavilion supported by ornamental pillars.[2]

---

[1] A. S. R. 1902–03, pp. 269–70.

[2] *Ib.* 1905–06, p. 15.

The Kingdom of Pāñcāla, famous as the premier one of India in the later years of the Vedic period, rose again to that proud position in the days of Harṣa (VIIth century) and of the Pratihāra emperors Mihira Bhōja and Mahēndrapāla (IXth century). Kanauj, the ancient Kānya Kubja, extending for about four miles along the east bank of the Gaṅgā, and adorned with lovely gardens and tanks of clear and sweet water, was its capital. It was ever the home of Vedic lore and its Brāhmaṇas were considered the bluest blooded in India. But its power waned in the Xth century; Rājyapāla was its King when Mahmūd appeared before Kanauj early in 1019 A.D. Rājyapāla made a feeble resistance and, though his capital had seven forts to protect it, let it fall into the Amīr's hands in the course of one day. Rājyapāla made an abject peace with the victor and retired to the opposite bank of the Gaṅgā, for which piece of cowardice he was severely punished by the other Hindu princes as will be presently narrated.

Jejābhukti, now known as Bundēlkhaṇḍ, lying between the Narmadā and the Yamunā, was ruled over by Kings of the Rājput clan of Candēllas, who waxed in strength as the power of Pāncāla waned in the Xth century. The strong fortress of Kālañjara was occupied by the Cañdēlla king, Yaśōvarmā in that century and this helped the dynasty to attain preeminence in North India and reduce the power of Pāncāla. Early in the XIth century the Cañdēlla capital was Khajurāho, "a wonderful town—furnished with big arches of great value", built in 1000 A.D. by Kōkalla, a petty chief and feudatory of the Candēllas, who also built there a temple of Vaidyanātha with "a lofty golden dome" and "a splendid canopy" for the god, and settled "a very learned crowd" of Brāhmaṇas near.[1] Meanwhile the fortress of Gōpādri (Gwalior), the ancient possession of the Pratihāras of Kanauj, was captured by Vajradāmā, head of Kacchapaghāta (Kacchvāha) clan, who became the feudatory of the Candēlla monarchs. Gaṇḍa, "the unrivalled hero" became its king in 1001 A.D. When Ānandapāla organized in vain a confederacy of Hindu princes in 1009 A.D. to oppose Mahmūd, it is said that Gaṇḍa sent a contingent. The cowardly surrender of Kanauj by Rājyapāla in 1019 A.D. encouraged Mahmūd to fall suddenly on Kālañjara, defeat the Candēlla general, Candra, and plunder the fortress. Thereupon Gaṇḍa organized a confederacy of Hindu princes to punish Rājyapāla. The head of the army sent for this purpose was his son Vidyādhara. Of this great prince it is said that he

> "gathered the flowers of the fame of his enemies" and "Bhōjadēva (of Dh rā) together with the Kalacuricandra, 'moon of the Kalacuris' (Gāṅgēyadēva), worshipped, full of fear, like a pupil, (this) master of warfare, who had caused the destruction of the king of Kānyakubja, and who was lying on a couch."[2]

Probably young Bhōja and Gāṅgēyadēva took part in awarding punishment to Rājyapāla. But the actual person who put an end to Rājyapāla's life was Arjuna, feudatory of the Candēllas. Vidyādhara was succeeded by Vijayapāladēva,

> "whose conquest of the world was stopped only by the ocean; when Gāṅgēyadēva, who had conquered the world, perceived before him (this) terrible one . . . the lotus of his heart closed the knot of pride in battle."[3]

---

[1] Ep. Ind. i. p. 152.

[2] *Ib.* i. p. 219.

[3] *Ib.* i. p. 219.

Read between the lines this merely means that Vijayapāladēva had no actual accomplishment to his credit. He was

> "eminent by widespreading fame (and) purifying conduct,"[1]

and quietly submitted to Bhōja.

Arjuna, the ruler of Gwalior, from 1004 A.D. to 1034 A.D., was

> "an ornament of the Kacchapaghāta family, (who) anxious to serve Vidyādharadēva, slew in battle Śrī Rājyapāla with many showers of arrows which pierced his neckbones."[2]

He was succeeded by his son, Abhimanyu. Of him it is said,

> "the celebrated King, Śrī Bhōja, has widely celebrated the skill which he showed in his marvellous management of horses and chariots and in the use of powerful weapons."[3]

In other words, he, too, acknowledged Bhōja as his suzerain lord.

At Kanauj, Rājyapāla was succeeded by Trilōcanapāladēva. He kept up the practice of bestowing gifts for the sake of spiritual benefit. In 1027 A.D. he resided near Prayāga and distributed a village among 6,000 Brāhmaṇas.[3] But the greatness of the Pratihāras was gone, never to return. The Paramāras, the Candēllas, the Kalacuris and even the Śōḷas of remote Tanjore interfered with the affairs of Kanauj and appointed governors from among their relatives to administer the states into which Kanauj was broken up. Adventurers set up independent government in parts of the province.

---

[1] Ep. Ind. i. p. 203.

[2] *Ib.* ii. p. 232–6.

[3] Ind. Ant. xviii. p. 34.

Thus in the Badāun (Vōdāmayūtā) district to the north of the Candēlla dominions was established a petty line of Rāṣṭrakūṭa kings in the XIth century by one Candra; this state soon became a bulwark capable of resisting the intrusion of the power of the Hambīras (Ghaznavīs) to the east of the Panjab.[1]

East of Sindh, south of the Panjab and the west of the Arāvallis in the desert region of Mārvāḍ, a branch of the Paramāra family ruled at Jālōr (Jābālapura). This family was exterminated when the Nadōḷ Cāhamāna Kīrttipāla made Jālōr his capital.

On Mount Ābū itself ruled the original branch of the Paramāra family with Candrāvatī as capital. Dandhuraja of this line averse from rendering homage to the Caulukya Bhīmadēva I, took refuge with Bhōjadēva. His son Kṛṣṇarāja was taken prisoner by Bhīma and held captive till he was compelled to release the Paramāra by Bālaprasāda, successor of Aṇahilla, the Cāhamāna chief of Mārvāḍ.[2]

On the eastern side of the Arāvallis was Mēvāḍ, where lived the Sisōdias, the purest-blooded amongst the Rājputs. There at Citōr or more properly Citōrgaḍh, on a long isolated hill lying above seventy miles to the east of modern Udaipur, was founded a city by Bappa, who was born in the forest to which his widowed mother had fled for refuge from a far-away corner of Kāthiāvāḍ, when her husband's kingdom was sacked and laid low and he died on the battle-field. The child grew to manhood among the wild Bhils and he became their chieftain and carved

---

[1] Ep. Ind. i. p. 64.

[2] *Ib.* xi. p. 68.

out for himself a kingdom around the impregnable rock of Citōr in the VIIIth century, and founded a house which has continued the Kṣattriya tradition unbroken to our own days. Bhōja's contemporaries among the princes of this house were Naravarmā and Kīrttivarmā, who were not very great monarchs.

To the north of the Arāvallis, still on high land is the lake of Sāmbhar (Sākambharī). In the district round this lake ruled the Cāhamāna (Cauhān) clan, destined to earn undying fame in the next century. The Cauhān contemporaries of Bhōja were Vākpati and Śrī Candra. From this Sākambharī family there branched off another line of Cāhamānas, which had its capital at Naddūḷa, the modern Nadōḷ, in the Jōdhpur state of Rājaputāna. The Naddūḷa chieftain at the beginning of the century was Ahila who fought with Bhīmadēva of Gujarāt. He was succeeded by his uncle, Aṇahilla. He continued the feud with Bhīmadēva, captured Sākambharī, killed Sāḍha, a general of Bhōjadēva, and defeated the Turuṣka King, Maḥmūd of Ghaznī in one of his raids.[1] The Cāhamānas of Nadōḷ exterminated the line of Paramāras of Mount Ābū at about the end of the century. Like the Paramāras of Candravatī, there was another minor branch of the family, which ruled over another part of Arbuda, Maṇḍala, the region round Mount Ābū. Pūrṇapāla of this branch was the contemporary of Bhōja and his widowed sister Lāhinī restored an ancient temple of the Sun and founded a tank (*vāpi*) in Vaṭa (Vasantagaḍh) east of Abū.[2]

To the west of Bhōja's dominions was the country of the Caulukyas (Sōḷaṅkis), which was called

[1] Ep. Ind. xi. pp. 68–9.

[2] *Ib.* ix. p. 11.

Gujarāt. Its capital was Aṇahilavāḍ. When the century began the Sōḷaṅki King was Cāmuṇḍadēva.

> "Inhaling even from afar the breeze perfumed with the ichor of his excellent elephants, Śrī Sindhurāja (of Mālva) fled together with his own elephants that were cowed by the smell of (their opponents,) rut and vanished in such wise that even the trace of the fame of that prince was lost." [1]

Before 1010 A. D. he was succeeded by his son Vallabharāja,

> "a crest-jewel among princes who astonished the circle of the earth by his bold deeds. Densely dark smoke, rising from the empire of the Mālva King, who quaked on hearing of his marching, indicated the spread of the fire of his anger." [1]

As already said, Vallabharāja died of small-pox when investing Dhārā. After him

> "ruled his brother, called Śrī Durlabharāja, who though his heart was bent on love, was not easily accessible (*durlabha*) to the wives of others. When filled with anger, he somewhat contracted his arched eyebrows, that forthwith indicated its result, the destruction of the Lāṭa country." [1]

After him ruled Bhīmadēva I, the great rival of Bhōja,

> "who, though terrible (*bhīma*) to his foes, ever granted enjoyments to his friends (and) as ruler, carried this load of the earth. What wonder was there that his horses supremely skilled in accomplishing the five paces (called *dhārā*) quickly gained Dhārā, the capital of the emperor of Mālva." [1]

This event as well as other dealings between Bhīma and Bhōja will be described in the next two chapters; but it may be mentioned here that Vimala Śā, general (*daṇḍanāyaka*) of Bhīma con-

---

[1] Ep. Ind. i, p. 302. Sindhurāja in this passage has been understood as 'King of Sindh.' We know of no such King in this period.

structed on Mount Ābū, one of the most beautiful of Indian temples in 1031 A.D. During Bhīma's reign Maḥmūd of Ghaznī is said to have done his final act of greatest daring—the dash on Sōmanātha in Gujarāt and the spoliation of its widely venerated temple. This event, Al 'Utbi, Maḥmūd's official biographer, though he lived after it is supposed to have taken place, does not mention; it is first described by Ibn Asrī, two hundred years after Maḥmūd's time. The rebuilding of the temple soon after Maḥmūd's supposed destruction of it is not mentioned in inscriptions, and it is impossible to believe the story that the hero-king of Gujarāt, the rival of Bhōja, fled at the approach of Maḥmūd and concealed himself in a distant fort when the Amīr leisurely plundered and destroyed the sacred fane.

At Valabhi, in a corner of Gujarāt there lived from the VIth century and perhaps much earlier a family of Maurya chiefs. They were great patrons of Brāhmaṇas. Of this family Bhailēka and Bhīmarāja were contemporaries of Bhōja.

Conterminous on the east with the dominions of Bhōja was the Kingdom of Cēdi, famous from the Vedic age. The Cēdis claimed descent from the Haihayas, famous warriors of the Vedic period. After that age the Haihaya clan never lost hold of Central India and under that name, or that of Cēdi or of Kalacuri exercised dominion there, which now powerful, now weak, never became quite extinct. The province was called Dāhala; Gāṅgēyadēva was its King in the beginning of the XIth century. Taking advantage of the decay of the power of the Pratihāras of Kanauj, he extended his sway to Prayāga and Kāsī in the South-eastern part of the empire over which the great Mihira Bhōja once ruled. Gāṅgēyadēva was "a thunderbolt falling on the heads of enemies, (and) the lord of the fortune of the heroes with a chest broad like an emerald tablet, (and) with smiling eyes, (and) with his two arms, surpassing the length of a city-bar, the crest-jewel of crowned heads, he has become famous under the name of Vikramāditya." [1]

Another inscription records that

"wishing to run away from him with dishevelled hair (the King of Kuntala) who was deprived of his country came to possess it again." [2]

Such conquest of provinces and restoration of them to defeated kings was a very common incident in Indian History, for kings then fought not to annex the countries of rival kings, but merely to prove on the field of battle their superior prowess. Like other kings of the age Gāṅgēyadēva was a builder of temples. He built "a *Mēru* without equal", *Mēru* being a hexagonal temple with twelve stories, variegated windows, and four entrances.[3] Gāṅgēyadēva was a great warrior; an inscription of the rival Candēlla royal house incidentally says that he "had conquered the world",[4] and Al Bērūnī mentions him in his *Indika*,[5] which means that Gāṅgēyadēva was so great a king that his fame reached the ears of that foreign writer. Gāṅgēyadēva was also a very pious person, for,

"fond of residing at the foot of the holy fig-tree of Prayāga, he found salvation there together with his hundred wives",[6]

by drowning in the holy waters of the three united streams, the Gaṅgā, the Yamunā and the concealed

---

[1] Ep. Ind. i. p. 6.

[2] *Ib.* xii. p. 215.

[3] *Ib.* ii. p. 15.

[4] Ep. Ind. i. p. 219.

[5] *Ib.* i. p. 212.

[6] *Ib.* xii. p. 215.

Sarasvatī. His son was Karṇa, the last of Bhōja's rivals, whose dealings with the lord of Mālva will be described in a subsequent chapter.

East of Benares, right up to Kāmarūpa (Assam), ruled at Muṅghyr Ma hīpala I and after him Nayapāla, devout princes who were Bauddhas and built temples of Śiva, Viṣṇu, and Sūrya and gave gifts to learned Brāhmaṇas, "for pleasing Gautama, the Saugata", who had about this time been recognized as an incarnation of Viṣṇu undertaken for the purpose of inculcation of mercy to animals and putting a stop to the wholesale slaughter of them in the name of the Vedic Yajña. The Pālas practised the Tāntrika rites which had, in later Buddhism, usurped the place assigned by the Buddha to ethical culture, and sent teachers of these practices to Tibet where they have found firm root. At the same time as the Pālas, other dynasties ruled over the outlying parts of Bengal. A family of kings whose names ended in Varmā held court at Siṁhapura in Rāḍha in the north of Bengal. Jaṭāvarmā, of this line, conquered a part of Kāmarūpa. He was the son-in-law of Karṇa of Cēdi. A line of Candras ruled at Candradvīpa in East Bengal. Govinda Candra of this house was the contemporary of Bhōja. Over Kāmarūpa proper ruled a family of kings whose names ended in—pāla, but who were different from the Great Pālas of Muṅghyr. Dharmapāla of this line reigned at the same time as Bhōja.

South of Bengal, in Orissa, the northernmost part of Trikaliṅga, which had absorbed its middle part, Koṅgōdha, and along with it a part of Mahākōsala to the west, was ruled over by the Kēsari line of Kings with Yayātinagar (now Jājnagar) as capital. In the early years of the XIth century, one Indraratha ruled at this place. The temple of

Jagannāth (Purī) was under the control of the Kēsaris and in those days in that temple Puruṣōttama (Viṣṇu) stood between a Śiva *linga* and a figure of Durgā.

South of the dominions of the Kēsaris was Kaliṅga proper, under the rule of the Gaṅgas, who had emigrated in the IVth century from Kōlāhala (Kōlār in Maisūr Province). These kings built numerous temples and Bhōja's contemporaries among them were Kāmārṇava and Vajrahasta III.

The Karṇāṭā Kingdom, as the dominions of the great line of the Western Cālukyas of Kalyāni was called, was, when the century began, under the rule of "the auspicious king of kings, supreme lord, supreme master, Akalaṅkacarita (of spotless conduct) Iṛivabedaṅga, (a wonder among those who pierced their foes), ornament of the Cālukya races, slayer of Tamils, the auspicious king Satyāśraya ".[1] He was frequently fighting with the great Tanjore Śōḻas and had generally the worst of it in those battles. One of his feudatories was Bhillama of Sēuṇadēśa, "ornament of the Yadu race, attended by the fortune of valour—. . . . (and) a pain in the head of the Mālavas "[2], for in the time of his former suzerain, he took Muñja captive in battle. Satyāśraya was succeeded by Vikramāditya V in 1009 A.D. and he ruled for two years. One of his feudatories was Iṛiva-Noḷambādhirāja, of a branch line which sprung from the great Pallavas of Kāñcī. After Vikramāditya V, ruled his brother, Jayasiṁha II Jagadēkamalla (the sole wrestler of the world). Among his feudatories were, besides Bhillama III, the Yādava, Cittarāja who was ruling over the whole of the Koṅkaṇ in 1026 A. D. and the Kādambas of

[1] Ep. Ind. xvi. p. 75. [2] Ep. Ind. xv. p. 37.

Goa. Jagdēkamalla had to fight with Rājēndra Śōḷa Parakēsari Varmā, who planted a column of victory in Kolhāpur in the Cālukya territory.[1] Jayasiṁha's relations with Bhōja will be described in the next Chapter. He was succeeded by his son, Sōmēśvara I Trailōkyamalla (the wrestler of the three worlds) and Āhāvamalla. He had numerous vassals, *viz.*, the Kādambas, the Śilāharas, the Sindas, etc. His relations with Bhōja will also be referred to in the next Chapter.

A branch of the Sinda family, belonging to the Nāgavaṁśa ruled over Bastar (in the Central Provinces). Their capital was Cakrakōṭa, which was captured by Rājēndra Śōḷa, who invested the Nāgavaṁśa King when the latter became his vassal, as was the custom in those days with his title of Madhurāntakadēva.

In South India proper (apart from the Deccan), from the banks of the Kṛṣṇā and the Tuṅgabhadrā to Cape Comorin, the power of the Tanjore Śōḷas was supreme. Rājarāja Rājakēsari, after a series of victories on land and sea established on firm foundations the Śōḷa power, built at Tanjore the temple of Bṛhadīśvara, the first temple built in India on a very large scale. In the second decade of the XIth century, he was succeeded by Rājēndra Parakēsari, who proved to be even a greater king than his father, and a greater warrior than the North Indian heroes of his time, Vidyādhara the Candēlla, Gaṅgēyadēva the Kalacuri, Bhōja the Paramāra and Bhīma the Sōḷaṅki. He conquered Iḍaituraināḍu in the Maisūr territory, Vanavāsi, the Kadamba province, Maṇṇaikkaḍakkam (Mānyakhēṭa), the capital of the Rāṣṭrakūṭas and the first of the later

[1] S. I. I. i. p. 133.

Cālukya emperors; then Ceylon and all the islands round the South Coast of India; then Iraṭṭaippāḍi, another part of the Cālukya dominions: he then started on a Napoleonic campaign towards the north; he captured Śakkarakkōṭṭam (Cakrakōṭa) and traversed Kaliṅga which submitted to him and defeated Indraratha, the Kēsari King of Ādinagaram (Yayātinagar); he subjugated Oḍḍaviṣayam (Orissa), Mahākōsala, Daṇḍabhukti (Mūrṣidābād Dt.), defeated Dharmapāla of Assam, Raṇaśūra, Govinda Candra and Mahipāla and thus Kāmarūpa, Rāḍha and Bengal lay at the feet of the conqueror. His influence reached Kanauj, where he set up one of his own men to 'rule' the country. He then assumed the title of *Gaṅgaikoṇḍa Śoḻa*, the Śōḻa who conquered (the region of) the Gaṅgā; he then founded a new capital, called Gaṅgai-kōṇḍa Śōḻapuram, not far from the mouth of the Coleroon, a branch of the Kāvēri, larger than the mother-river, and a royal palace five miles in circuit. Near his palace he built a temple on the same scale as that of his father at Tanjore and installed there a *lingam*, which well deserves its name of *Bṛhadīśvara*, the Great Lord, being thirty-six feet tall. He also built a large fresh water lake called *Ponnēri*, the golden lake and sanctified it by having several pots of holy Gaṅgā water, sent to him daily by his northern feudatories, poured into it. He then enlarged his fleet, invaded Burma and compelled the kings of Burma, Siam and Jāva to acknowledge his sway. His inscriptions range from Kaliṅga to Siam. Verily in the first half of the XIth century India was the land of giants!

CHAPTER V

BHŌJA'S WARS

It was the fashion in those days for each great Rājā to keep fighting with other great Rājās, opponents worthy of carrying on passages of arms with them. The motive of these wars was not so much to annex any portion of the territories of his neighbours as to prove the king's prowess and to assert his claim to the more or less empty title of the *Cakravartī*, Supreme lord of Bhāratavarṣa. These Rājās loved to include, in their official documents, grandiloquent phrases indicative of their superiority to others and describing the successes achieved by them in battle and the acts of charity done by them. From these phrases the history of India from the age of the Mauryas almost up to that of the establishment of the British Empire can be reconstructed. But often these epigraphs contain vague self-laudatory statements, conventional phrases, meaning nothing in particular. As a rule, eulogies, which are only exercises in general flattery and do not mention facts, have to be separated from definite statements of historical events and treated as useless for purposes of history.

The *Prabandhas* or chronicles, composed centuries after the death of the kings whose life-stories they propose to deal with, contain accounts of historical events, but also include anachronistic anecdotes and also conventional hyperbolic phrases of praise which cannot be accepted as sober history. As an instance of the anachronistic statements of the *Prabandhas*, it may be mentioned that they relate how, to avenge the savage treatment of his uncle,

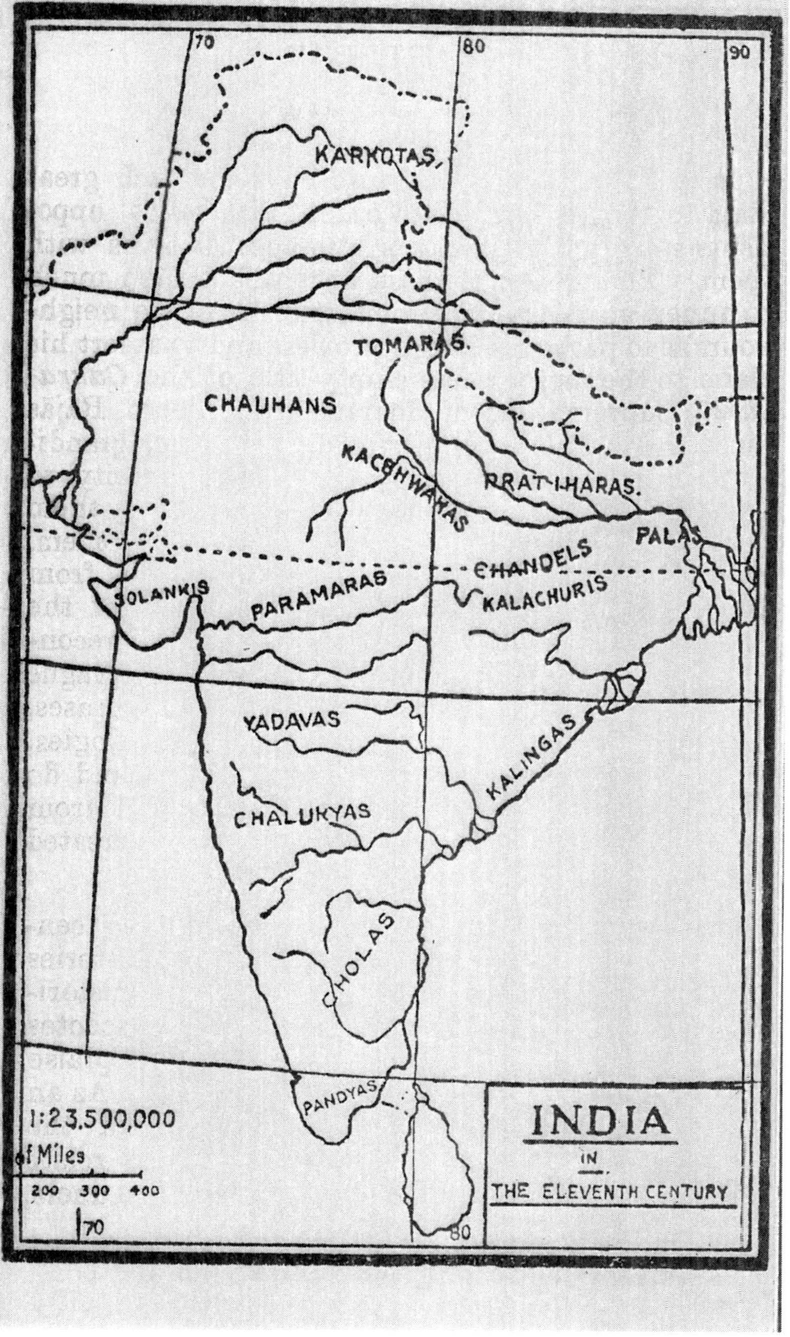

70
80
90
KARKOTAS
TOMARAS
CHAUHANS
KACHHWAHAS
PRATIHARAS
PALAS
CHANDELS
SOLANKIS
PARAMARAS
KALACHURIS
YADAVAS
KALINGAS
CHALUKYAS
CHOLAS
PANDYAS
1:23,500,000
f Miles
200 300 400
70
80
INDIA
IN
THE ELEVENTH CENTURY

Muñja by Tailapa II, Bhōja invaded the Deccan, captured Tailapa and subjected him to the same indignities as were loaded on Muñja's head. This cannot be true, for Tailapa died several years before Bhōja ascended the throne. But other statements in the *Prabandhas* are corroborated by the contemporary testimony of inscriptions; yet others are so probable, so consonant with what we know of the character of Bhōja and his times, that we can accept them as true even without other evidence to confirm them. But some scholars have pursued the dangerous game of extracting, by *a priori* methods, the possible kernel of truth from manifestly impossible stories and have guessed that Bhōja may have defeated Vikramāditya V, the weak successor of Tailapa and visited the son with punishment for the sins of his parent;[1] this cannot be accepted as true, for there is not the least indication anywhere else to show that there was any war between the Paramāras and the Cālukyas between 997 A. D. and 1019 A. D.

The earliest reference to Bhōja in Deccan epigraphs occurs in the Kādamba inscription of Irivabeḍangadēva, lord of Banavāse and feudatory of the Cālukya Emperor, Jayasiṁha II Jagadēkamalla; in this inscription Irivabedangadēva calls his Suzerain, Jayasiṁha, '*bhōjanṛpāmbhōja rājan ina nibha tējan*',[2] *i.e*, a moon (*rājan*) to the lotus (*ambhōja*) which was King Bhōja, glorious (*tējan*) as the Sun (*nibha ina*). Such vague praises of kings and generals accompanied by dispraises of their traditional enemies, without the mention of particulars of battles, were common in those days

---

[1] E. H. D. p. 64 Ind. Ant. xlviii, pp. 117-8.

[2] Ind. Ant. v. p. 15.

and mean nothing. Thus Kundiga (Kundamarasa), son of Irivabedaṅgadēva Satyāśraya, and cousin of Jayasiṁha and feudatory governor of Banavāse was thus praised in one inscription.

> "O Kundiga, when they name thee in respect of courage, what further praise can others give? Is it not what is said by the troops of elephants of the Cōla, the Gāṅgēya (and) king Bhōja with open mouths as they flee away in a battle where they are pressed by (thy) elephants furious with storms of rutting ichor, as they flee away in terror, through which they gallop off without waiting at all to charge with their tusks?" [1]

Nothing can be inferred from this.

In a later passage of the former inscription there occurs what seems to be a definite statement of fact with regard to Jayasiṁha's fight with Bhōja. As translated by the editor of the inscription, it says that Jayasiṁha

> "searched out and beset and pursued and ground down and put to flight the confederacy of Mālva"; [2]

from this it has been inferred that Bhōja organized a league against Jayasiṁha, but was completely defeated by the Cālukya emperor. The passage, properly translated, means,—

> "The rising of the glory of Jayasiṅgadēva has curbed (or destroyed) the seven Mālavas (*Māḷavam ēḷumam*) in such a way that they have to be searched for" [3]

---

[1] Ep. Ind. xv. p. 333.

[2] Ind. Ant. v. p. 17.

[3] The original has *Māḷavamēḷumam puḍuke gattiśidattu etc.* Mr. H. Sesha Iyengar, Fellow in Canarese, Madras University, informs me that *Māḷavamēḷumam* is *Māḷavam ēḷumam*, *i.e.*, 'Mālavas even seven' and not *Māḷava mēḷa*, i.e., Mālava confederacy.' 'The rising of the glory', the subject of the sentence occurs lower down; it is *tējadurbu*, I.A. v. p. 16, l. 2.

Since the middle of the VIIth century, Mālva was divided into seven little states, frequently mentioned in inscriptions as the *Sapta Māḷavas.* The Pratihāras on the one hand and more often the Rāṣṭrakūṭas on the other raided the seven Māḷavas and annexed some of the states. Thus Dantidurga subjugated the Māḷavas; [1] hence the destruction of the seven Māḷavas was one of the great deeds attributed to the Rāṣṭrakūṭas and the Cālukyas who succeeded to the titles as well as the dominions of the former. Nothing more is meant by the phrase. Long before Jayasiṁha's time, *i.e.*, ever since Upēndra conquered Mālva, it was a well-knit kingdom and the phrase 'Mālva confederacy' became meaningless, nor were there at that time seven great powers near Mālva, who could form a confederacy.

The *Prabandhas* themselves indicate that Bhōja did not invade the Deccan in hot haste, soon after his coronation. He seems to have forgotten the duty of punishing the Cālukyas, and, on the other hand, been more anxious to establish by force of arms his superiority to his great rival of Gujarāt, Bhīmadēva. The story goes that in a certain year, owing to the failure of rain, it was impossible in Gujarāt to obtain grain for men to eat, nor grass for horses or cattle, and at the same time King Bhōja was preparing for an invasion of the country. Bhīma heard of this and being unprepared for fighting with the mighty lord of Mālva, sent word to Ḍāmara (Dāmōdara), his diplomatic agent at Dhārā, to prevent the invasion at that juncture, if necessary, by paying a fine to Bhōja. Ḍāmara, ugly-looking but extremely clever, presented himself before the King, who accosted him with,—

> "Tell me how many messengers are there, belonging to your king, holding the office of diplomatic agent?"

---

[1] I.A. xi. p. 108, Ellora Insc. A.S.W.I., v. 87.

Ḍāmara replied,—

"Many like me, O Mālva king, they are of three degrees
As foreign courts are low or medium or high in rank."

The king of Dhārā then ordered the drums to be beaten as a signal for the army to march on Gujarāt. A poet stood in front of the king and proclaimed,

"The Sōḻa is entering the bosom of the great sea
The Āndhra is hiding in caves of the mountains,
The king of Karṇāṭa is standing bareheaded,
The Gūrjara Rājā has fled to the torrents,
The Warrior monarch of Cēdi is trembling,
The Lord of Kanauj is bent double with terror,
O Bhōja, the fear of thy army alarms all.
The floor of thy prison is crowded with princes;
They are fighting for places for spreading their beds on,
'When a new one arrives there, an inmate exclaims loud,
The Koṅkaṇa sleeps in a corner, the Lāṭa,
At the door, the Kaliṅga does lie in the courtyard;
You, Kōsala lord, just arrived here, my father,
Did use to abide on this level spot here, Sir'".

This kind of laudation was in those days thought to be proper when offered by poets to kings, and as in every royal court it was indulged in, and it was the acknowledged convention of darbārs, it was not considered to be bad manners or the expression of haughtiness.

Before the army actually started, a drama was enacted in the royal presence, taking off all the kings of the time. One of the scenes was laid in a prison, where Tailapa had established himself in a comfortable corner. A new arrival tried to make Tailapa give up the cosy spot, but Tailapa replied to him,—

"This corner is my heritage from great
Fobears, shall I resign my ancient home
To you who have arrived but yesterday?"

Bhōja was pleased with the flattery implied and, turning to Ḍāmara with a smile, asked him if it was not a very witty play. Ḍāmara said in reply,

> "The wit is there all right, but this fool of Tailapa holds the head of thy uncle fixed on a stake."

Stung to the quick, because he was thus cleverly reminded of the disgraceful treatment undergone by Munja which he had apparently forgotten, Bhōja gave up the design of subjugating Gujarāt and went straight against the Cālukya territory. He marched south along the coast to Koṅkaṇa, which was a part of the dominions of Jayasiṁha, grandson of Tailapa.

Arikēsarī, *alias* Kēsīdēva, feudatory of Jayasiṁha II, was then the ruler of Northern Koṅkaṇa. He belonged to the clan of the Śilāhāras. The clan was so called because its members claimed to be descended from Jīmutavāhana, the hero of the Saṁskṛta drama, the *Nāgānandam*. Jīmutavāhana lay on a rock (*silā*) as food (*āhāra*) for Garuḍa in order to save a victim destined for the divine bird and hence Jīmutavāhana's descendants called themselves *Śilāhāras*, (food on the rock) and carried as an emblem of this a Golden Garuḍa-banner, (*suvarṇa garuḍa dhvaja*). Their capital was a town named Purī, very near modern Bombay. Bhōja gained a victory in the Northern Koṅkaṇa and captured the province.

Two of the three inscriptions of Bhōja discovered so far, refer to the war with the Cālukyas. One was issued on the fifth day (*tithi*) of the bright fortnight of the month of Māgha, in 1019 A. D. It is signed "in the own hand of Śrī Bhōjadēva" (*Svahastōyam srībhōjadevasya*). In it he informs all royal officers (*rājapuruṣān*) coming to Vaṭapadraka included in the Ghāgradōra District (*bhōga*) of the Sthalī province (*maṇḍala*), and the Brāhmaṇas and other inhabitants,

> "On (the occasion) of the festival (*parvaṇi*) celebrating the conquest of Konkaṇa, I have bathed and worshipped the lord of the moving and the motionless, Bhagavān Bhavānipati, and considered the worthlessness of worldly life: it has been said, the rule of the earth is as shifting as the clouds beaten about by the winds; the enjoyments of objects is pleasant only at the moment when they are obtained; life is like the drop of water at the tip of grass; *dharma* is the best companion on the way to the other world. Wealth streams away like the water flowing from the rim of the wheel of *Saṁsāra* (when it runs on a flooded road); repentance, therefore, is the fruit obtained by one who does not give it away (in charity). I have considered the changing nature of the world and granted 100 *nivarttanas*[1] of land in the above mentioned village to the Brāhmana Bhāila, son of Vāmana, of the Vasiṣṭha *gōtra*, and of the Vāji-Mādhyandina *śākhā*, whose ancestors had emigrated from Chincha city (*sthāna*)." [2]

In the same year,[3] a few months later, *i.e.*, in the month of Bhādrapada, on the fifteenth day of the bright fortnight, Bhōjadēva gave the village of Nāḷataḍāga, one of the seventeen villages of the Nyāyapadra sub-division to a Brāhmaṇa named Paṇḍita Delha, son of Bhaṭṭa Ṭaṭṭhaśikh, of the Kauśika *gōtra* and of the Mādhyandina *śākhā*, who came from Sthāṇvīśvara and whose ancestors had come from the village of Viśālagrāma. The occasion of the gift was the celebration of the victorious occupation of Konkaṇa, (*Konkaṇa-grahaṇa vijaya parvaṇi*).[4] Konkaṇa then was included in Bhōja's

---

[1] A *nivarttana* is a square piece of land, each arm measuring 200 cubits.

[2] Ind. Ant. vi. 53.

[3] The year began not with Caitra but with Kārtika.

[4] Ep. Ind. xviii. p. 321.

dominions for some time. Koṅkaṇa recovered its independence a little while after, for in the year 1026 A. D., Chittarāja, a Śilāhāra chief, was described as ruling the whole of Koṅkaṇa,[1] though this is not decisive evidence that Bhōja lost all control over the province he conquered.

The feud with the Cālukyas did not end with the punishment inflicted on Koṅkaṇa. Sōmēśvara I ascended the Cālukya throne in 1042 A.D. Bilhaṇa, Court-poet of his son, Vikramaditya VI, and author of the poem *Vikramāṅkadēvacaritam* refers in a few *ślōkas* to Sōmēśvara's campaign against Dhārā. Speaking of Sōmēśvara I, Bilhaṇa in a passage, filled with the quaint conceits, fashionable in that period, describes him as a king,

> "whose sword, appearing thirsty owing to the nearness of the blazing fire of his valour, swallowed the noble (city of) Dhārā, which was the *dhārā* (stream) of the renown of the Pramāra (Paramāra) lord of the earth,
>
> whose sword, even after drowning many royal families in abysmal waters, could not, owing to the decline of the fortunes of the King of Mālva, stop short of capturing the sole (unparalleled city of) Dhārā,
>
> who, having completely defeated the royal swans (the best kings) by his sword, dark (powerful) as the young (newly risen) cloud, killed the swan of the fame, which was encaged (as it were) in the arms of King Bhōja,
>
> whose fierce fire of heroism, glowing in battles, which was like the fire that consumes the universe at the time of its destruction (*Kālāntakālāgni*), was quenched wonderfully (quickly) when he plunged into the (*dhārā*) stream (i.e., entered into the city of Dhārā) deserted by King Bhōja."[2]

Bilhaṇa in this passage does not wholly indulge in a conventional praise of the father of his hero. For in an inscription of a general of this Sōmēśvara I,

---

[1] Ind. Ant. v. p. 278.

[2] Bil. Vik. Car. i. 91–4.

Trailōkyamalla Vallabha, he is described as "a shatterer of the pride of the potent Cōḷa monarch, a submarine fire to the whole of the ocean that is the race of the Māḷavyas." [1] In the same inscription Nāgadēva, the general, who was the steward of the household (*śrīman mane verggade daṇḍanāyaka*) is called 'a Garuḍa to the serpent Bhōja' (*bhōja-bhujangāhidviśa*).[2] In another inscription, another general of Sōmēśvara, the *Mahāmaṇḍalēśvara* Jēmarasa, is described as 'a flame of doom to Bhōja,' (*bhōjakālānala*). Hence it may be concluded that Sōmēśvara did raid Bhōja's capital, probably at a time when Bhōja was engaged outside his province in one of his smaller wars.

The greatest rival of Bhōjadēva was Bhīmadēva of Aṇahilavāḍ. In the matter of skill in war, of patronage of scholars, earnest discharge of the duties of religion, and of the building of temples and other charitable institutions, Bhīma aimed at gaining as much reputation as Bhōja. Bhōja's desire to humble Bhīma has already been referred to. After his conquest of Końkaṇa, his mind reverted to his desire of punishing Bhīma for the sin of the latter's father, in invading Mālva and investing the fort of Dhārā to the great distress of Bhōja's father, Sindhurāja. Bhīma, on the other hand, was itching for an opportunity for taking arms against Bhōja. But there existed a league of peace between the two great kings. Being desirous of breaking the peace and wishing at the same time to test the cleverness of the poets of Gujarāt, Bhōja composed a *gāthā* to the following effect,—

"The lion who cleaves with ease the heads of elephants, whose might is noised abroad,

---

[1] Ep. Ind. xv. p. 87-8.

[2] *Ib.* xvi. p. 83.

> Deigns not to fight with the deer, yet none can truly say, he keeps with him in peace" :

and sent it to Bhīma by means of a diplomatic agent. Bhīma got one of his poets to compose this retort,—

> "Bhīma by fate created to destroy the sons of Andhaka
> Can he who fought with hundred foes now shrink from thee who are but one?"

This exchange of *gāthās* did not serve to cool the military ardour of Bhōja.

Another incident whetted his appetite for war. Ḍāmara, the diplomatic agent of Bhīma at the court of Dhārā, would often paint in pleasing phrases the beauty of Bhīma's person and rouse in Bhōja's mind a longing to see the King of Gujarāt. When Ḍāmara returned to Aṇahilavāḍ, he described in such glowing terms the splendour of the court of Dhārā, that Bhīma wished to observe it with his own eyes. But the rigid etiquette of courts and the fear of treachery stood in the way of the accomplishment of the desire of the princes to meet each other. Ḍāmara, wily as all successful diplomats have to be, found occasion to convey from the Sōḷaṅki court costly presents to Bhōja and took with him Bhīma disguised as a betel-bearer, the inevitable attendant of princes and nobles. Then King Bhōja hinted that Ḍāmara might bring to his court the king of Gujarāt, and Ḍāmara replied,—

> "Kings are independent persons. Who can force them to do what they do not wish to do? But, still, some servants may not be despised by Your Majesty."

Then Bhōja asked him how old Bhīma was and what his colour and form were like, and looked round at the people who were present in the court. Ḍāmara pointed to the betel-bearer and said,—

> "He has the same shape, the same colour, the same beauty, and the same age; the difference between him and the king is that between glass and a wishing jewel."

Then Bhōja, master of the science, among others, of physiognomy, saw through the disguise and concluded that the betel-bearer was king Bhīma. Ḍāmara, scenting danger to his royal master, at once ordered the betel-bearer to go to his quarters and bring the rest of the presents intended for the king of Dhārā. Then Ḍāmara, to gain time, began to describe, in a dilatory fashion, the excellences of the gifts already presented and to discuss other subjects. Bhōja then impatiently demanded,—

> "How much longer is your betel-bearer going to linger?"

Ḍāmara, suppressing a smile, replied,—

> "At the end of every twelve *yōjanas* from Dhārā to Aṇahilavāḍa stand horses ready littered; camels can go a *yōjana* in one Indian hour (of twenty-four minutes)."

Then Bhōja realized that he had been cleverly outwitted and that Bhīma had fled to the capital of Gujarāt, fearing possible treachery at the hands of his rival. Some time after this, Bhīma started on an expedition to Sindh and Bhōja ordered his Commander-in-chief, Kulacandra, to invade the dominions of the Sōḷaṅkis.

An interesting story is related about the circumstances which led to the appointment of Kulacandra as the general of Bhōja's army. The king, as was his wont, was wandering about the town, after the general assembly in the evening had been dissolved. He then heard a Digambara Jaina reciting the following *gāthā*,—

> "A failure is this birth of mine,
> No sword of foe have I yet smashed;
> Shrill sounding drums have I not heard,
> Nor clung to neck of lady fair."

The man thus regretted that he had had no opportunities of realizing either object of life, love or war, *Agam* or *Puṛam*, as they are called in ancient

Tamil poems. The king sent for the man the next morning, reminded him of the *gāthā* he had uttered the previous night and asked him what he could achieve. He replied by means of a couplet,—

> "After the feast of the Row of Lamps is o'er, when elephant's ichor flows,
>
> Within thy one umbrella will I bring Dakṣiṇāpatha and Gauḍa."

Dakṣiṇāpatha meaning the country to the south of the Vindhyas and Gauḍa, that to the north. He was thereupon appointed commander-in-chief.

In the cold weather, when Bhīma was away in the region of the Sindhu, Kulacandra proceeded to Gujarāt, captured the august city of Aṇahilavāḍ, caused cowries to be sown at its gates and extorted a *Jayapatra*, a letter acknowledging his victory written by the general in charge of the town. When he returned to Dhārā and reported what he had done, Bhōja jokingly remarked,—

> "The taxes of this country (paid in cowries by the poor) shall go to Gujarāt. Why did you not have charcoal sown?"

Most probably an iron *Jayasthambha*-pillar was set up in Dhārā in honour of the victory obtained by Kulacandra, which will be described in a later chapter.

Kulacandra had acquired one object of life, success in war; the other desire of his remained to be accomplished. One night when he was sitting in the company of Bhōja, bathed in the cool rays of the full moon, the king recited the first half of a stanza,—

> "Speedily flits the night like a short minute
> When the beloved one is sitting beside thee;
> Seated apart from her, lonely, you feel that
> Cold-rayed the moon may be, but yet she scorches."

Kulacandra completed this with an appropriate half-stanza,—

"Know I not either the love of a lady
Nor have I suffered the sorrow of parting;
Having no knowledge of loving or losing
Mirror-like, neither hot nor yet cold shines she."

When he heard this, the king bestowed a beautiful damsel on Kulacandra.

Besides these great wars, Bhōja must have been engaged in a number of petty wars, but there is no record of these available. Some of the wars were conducted not by him in person, but by his generals. Thus from an inscription of the Naddūḷa Cāhamānas we learn that a general (*daṇḍādhīśa*) of Bhōjadēva's, called Sāḍha, was defeated or slain by Aṇahilla, son of Mahēndra of Naddūḷa.[1] Bhōja must have overthrown these and several other petty chiefs before they acknowledged him as their liege lord and he was hailed as supreme among the kings of India. Another inscription says that Bhīmadēva I tried to compel Dhandurāja of the branch of the Paramāra clan that ruled with Candravatī as capital, to become his vassal, but the Paramāra chief, averse from paying homage to the Caulukya, took refuge at Dhārā[2] The military activities of Bhōja must then have been frequent, for in the first half of the XIth century, jealousies among the Rājaput chiefs were rife and without ceaseless resort to arms, the lord of Dhārā could not have maintained his status as the premier one among the Rājās of the time.

The Udēpur *praśasti* sums up the military activities of Bhōja in one *ślōka* :—

---

[1] Ep. Ind. ix, p. 72, xi. p. 68.

[2] *Ib*. i. p. 238.

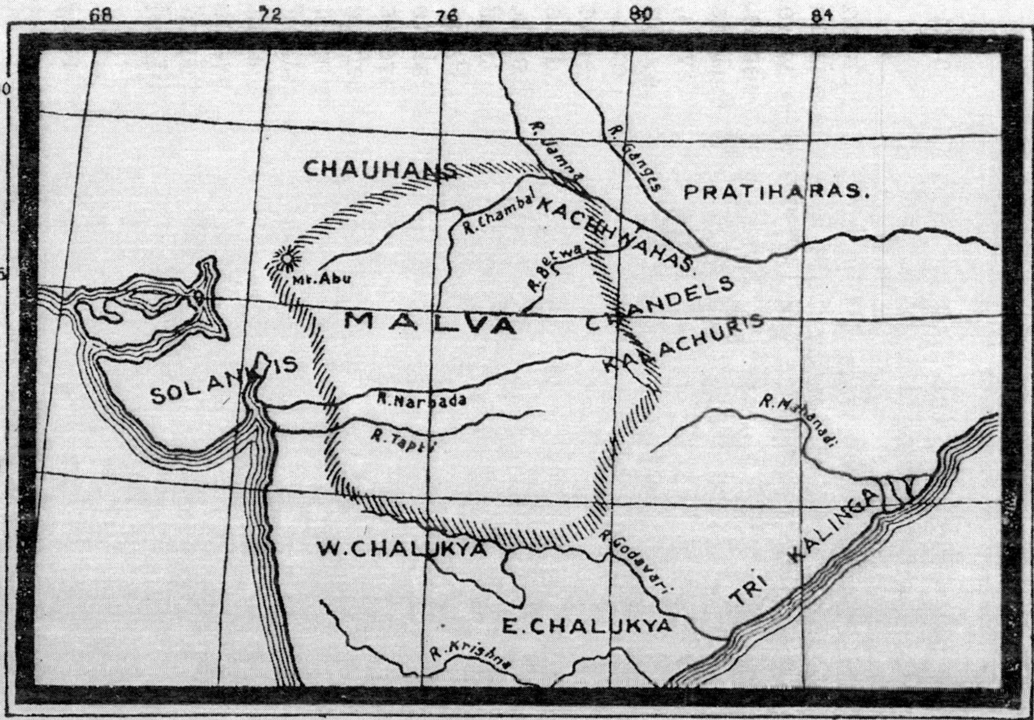

Bhōja's Dominions.

"Seeing the Karnāṭas, the lord of Lāṭa, the king of Gūrjara, the Turuṣkas, chief among whom were the lord of Cēdi, Indraratha, Toggala, and Bhīma, conquered by his mercenaries alone, his hereditary warriors thought only of the strength of their arms, not of the numbers of the fighters." [1]

In the *Pārijātamañjarī* of *Vijayaśrī*, a *nāṭikā* (a drama of four acts) by Madana, a Gauḍa (Bengal) Brāhmaṇa and preceptor (*Rājaguru*) of Arjunavarmā (a descendant of Bhōja, and king of Mālva in the first two decades of the XIIIth century), recently discovered, engraved on a slab of black stone at Dhārā in the Bhōja Śālā (now Kamal Maula Mosque), there occurs a *praśasti*. It says,

"Victorious is Kṛṣṇa: like Kṛṣṇa, Arjuna; and like Arjuna, the glorious king Bhōjadēva, who was able to defeat (his enemies) by leaping arrows; who afforded protection to the whole earth; who assumed the *rādhā* (a particular attitude in shooting, being that of standing with the feet a span apart, the shooting from which is called *rādhāvēdha*, in which Arjuna was proficient), which distressed (his enemies) by wounds from roaring, terrible arrows; and who had his desires speedily fulfilled for a long time at the festive defeat of Gāṅgēya." [2]

The latter part of the stanza, which has a double meaning, has to be translated in the case of Kṛṣṇa,

"who was able to defeat the leaping (demon) Bāṇa; who afforded help to all the cows (by lifting up the mountain Gōvarddhana); who made Rādhā distressed by being smitten by manifest love." [3]

The last phrase implies that Bhōja defeated the Kalacuri King Gāṅgēya, as Arjuna defeated Bhīṣma, the son of Gaṅgā; but this is merely a piece of flattery, there being no other evidence to show that Gāṅgēya Dēva and Bhōja fought with each other.

---

[1] Ep. Ind. i. p. 238.

[2] A. S. R. 1903-04, p. 241.

[3] Ep. Ind. viii. p. 93.

CHAPTER VI

BHŌJA, THE MAN

Pessimism in India, especially in the part of the country north of the Vindhyas, seems to be the result of the action, on the minds of men, of the environment in which they had to live. The vast scale in which objects have been made by Nature—the towering Hīmālayas, with their grand glaciers and other destructive agencies, the broad-bosomed rivers, the Sindhu, the Gaṅgā and the Brahmaputra, whose floods destroy, not isolated villages and towns, but envelop at one stroke large and populous districts, the earthquakes which lay low immense structures and crack the surface of the earth for many miles, the monsoon storms which lift tall and heavy buildings and toss them afar, as easily as birds of prey lift and toss rats and vermin, the rains which ruin the crops of wide acres of cultivated lands, the forest fires which easily consume many miles of thickly wooded tracts—these fill the mind of man with the deep sense of human helplessness in the fight with nature's forces of destruction, and of the transitoriness of all earthly life and the enjoyments the world has to offer. Thus, in the lives of even the least advanced races such as the Nāgas of Assaṁ, which one would expect to be marked by the spontaneous geniality bred from continuous sensuous enjoyment uninhibited by the melancholy of the cultured philosopher, there runs a deep vein of sadness.

> "The thought of death is never far from them and the fear of it is a potent factor in their lives. . . There is a tendency in the vast majority of their songs to animadvert on the brevity of life and finality of death." [1]

---

[1] Hood, Prim. Cult. Ind. p. 45 (quoting from Hutton).

The endless holocausts at the gorgeous sacrifices offered by kings at the latter half of the Vedic period and the frightful slaughter of men on the field of Kurukṣētra during the Armageddon of the Mahābhārata, intensified this age-long Indian outlook on life. Brāhmaṇa sanyāsīs renounced the world and its ways, eagerly seeking for the permanent release from the necessity of leading incarnate lives of mixed joy and sorrow. The Āgama, the Jaina, and especially the Bauddha cults opened the door of renunciation to men and women of all castes and of all grades of society alike. Ultimately, the eloquent exposition of the Advaita Vēdānta, though intended primarily for Brāhmaṇa Sanyāsīs, carried this sense of the vanity of earthly life, this feeling that all joys turn into pain at the moment of enjoyment, all fruits turn into dust in the mouth, into the minds of householders (*Gṛhastas*) and pessimism began to reign in the hearts of prince and peasant alike. This was accentuated by the frequent wars which the morbid sense of honour felt by Rājaput princes led them to and the consequent changes in their fortunes. Bhōja, the greatest scholar of his age, steeped in the immense philosophical literature produced during almost two millenniums before his time, and the greatest warrior of the century who had tasted catastrophic reverses of fortune since his boyhood, always carried with him the thought that life and its enjoyments were uncertain as the waves of the sea. He would frequently repeat to himself the following stanza:—

> "If men but saw the hand of death impending o'er their heads,
> E'en food would give no joy, much less the deeds that are not right."

The remarks and quotations embodied in the copperplate grant quoted in p. 50 show how the sense of the transitoriness of all things had burnt itself deep into the soul of Bhōja.

One day [1] when he was sitting on his throne in the Hall of Audience, he put into his mouth and devoured a betel-leaf which his betel-bearer had given to him, without waiting for the spiced areca-nut to be handed over. His courtiers were surprised at this unusual proceeding and he explained it as follows :—

> "As men are always between the teeth of death, what they give and what they enjoy may alone be said to be their own; about the rest there is a doubt."

Therefore, on getting up from bed each day a man must ask himself, 'what good can I do today?'

> "The sun will set in the western sky and take away with him a part of life.
> Men ask me daily 'what's the news today, are you quite hale and glad and fit?'
> How can we keep the body's health? Is not our life departing day by day?"

> "Perform today the duty of tomorrow, the afternoon's, before the noon;
> For death won't wait to see if you have done the duty of the day or no.
> Is death now dead, is eld now decrepit, are life's disasters now destroyed?
> The rush of illness quite arrested, that all these men are lost in mirth?"

One poet well understood the king's bent of mind and said,—

> "Well mounted on a steed that's moving fast, the Lord of Death is nearing you,
> Hence always you must be engaged, my lord, in following the path of Dharma."

[1] These anecdotes, as well as many in the preceding and succeeding chapters, are taken with slight alterations from Mērutuṅga's *Prabandhacintāmaṇi*, as translated by C. H. Tawney.

The king gave daily an appropriate gift to the author of this stanza.

Filled with these thoughts Bhōja would go daily to the 'pavilion of distribution' and bestow gold on petitioners waiting at his gate and summoned one after another by his attendants. It is said that he had, engraved on the bracelets that he wore, *ślōkas* to the following effect:—

"Uncertain by nature is human prosperity,
The time of possession is the time for bestowal;
Misfortune is certain to reach you quite soon,
Too late to discover a chance for well-doing?
O, full moon! now paint white the wide world all over; with bright beams abounding, the full wealth thou possessest;
Accursed is fate who will suffer no part of thy riches to stay here established for long.
O lake, now is the time for thy aiding suppliants with ceaselessly flowing rich streams of thy waters;
Moreover now water is easy to get, for not long since the clouds sailed aloft in the heavens,
For but a brief time does the flood stay, though mounting to great heights when currents were flowing quite fiercely;
The mischief the flood does remain long, it lays low the tall trees that grace both the banks of the river.'"

Bhōja had, also, incised like a charm on his necklet, a stanza composed by himself and containing the following sentiment:—

"If I have not given my wealth to suppliants before the bright sun does set in the west,
Can any one man that is living assure me to whom this my wealth will belong on the morrow."

This habit of giving away his wealth to those that sought it became really a vice and made wide holes in the royal treasury. His minister Rōhaka was alarmed but could not summon enough courage to protest to the king in person, against the extravagance of the royal gifts; so he wrote at night with chalk on the notice-board of the pavilion, a part of a *ślōka* which ran thus:—

"One ought to keep his wealth against the day of want."

The king, next morning, happened to notice this hemistich and wrote underneath,—

"How can calamity befall a lucky man?"

The minister wrote thereunder,—

"At times, in sooth, does Destiny with anger rage."

The king then wrote in reply, in the presence of the minister,—

"Then truly vanish piled-up heaps of gold,"

Thus completing the couplet, and said to Rōhaka,—

"Even men like the prime minister cannot restrain the elephant of my resolution with the elephant-hook (*aṅkuśa*) of wisdom."

The artistic sense of Indian princes made them adorn their persons and their clothes profusely with gold and the 'nine gems', but this pomp and circumstance did not isolate them from the common people; for the Rājā was accessible to the poorest of his subjects as some of the above anecdotes show. Besides, they were always in the habit of wandering far and near both by day and by night, for the purpose of acquainting themselves with the condition of their subjects, their wants and disabilities. On one such occasion in the winter season, when he was walking in front of a temple he heard a certain man reciting stanzas to the following effect:—

"The fire in my belly pinched with hunger, it blows and parts my lips, but is quenched,
When I'm shrivelled up like the fruit of the bean and plunged deep in a sea of care;

> But sleep has abandoned me and gone far away, like an insulted wife.
>
> The night doesn't quickly waste away like wealth betowed on a worthy man."

The king summoned the distressed wit the next morning and asked him,

> "How did you endure the severe cold the rest of the night?"

and quoted the last line of the stanza which the man had recited. He replied,

> "By virtue of the three thick garments I managed to hold out against the cold."

The king then asked him,

> "What is this triad of garments that you speak of?"

The reply came in the form of a couplet,

> "At night the knee, by day the sun, the fire at both twilights,
>
> O king, did I endure the cold by knee and sun and fire."

The king gave him a large present for this sally of wit.

The most ordinary citizens, even those who followed professions considered to be very low, could rebuke the king if they thought themselves called upon to do so. Bhōja desired to master the *rādhā vēdha* and secured proficiency in that feat of archery by dint of constant practice. So great did the king regard the accomplishment that he ordered the city to be illuminated in honour of the event; but an oilman and a tailor refused to take part in the rejoicings. On the contrary the oilman stood in the upper room of his house and, to caricature the *rādhā vēdha*, he poured from the upper storey a stream of oil without spilling a drop, into the narrow mouth of an earthen pot placed in the street. The tailor stood on the ground and, on the point of an uplifted thread, caught the eye of a needle thrown down from above and so threaded the needle. In this manner they cut short the king's pride.

Another story shows how freely the king moved with his subjects. One of the reasons why old Indian kings wandered through the streets at nights disguised, was that they thereby got into touch with popular opinion on the king's administration. One night, roaming about with a friend he was afflicted with thirst. The house of a *hetaera* happened to be near; they entered it and the friend asked for water on behalf of the king. The woman readily brought a cocoanut-shell filled with sugarcane juice and apologetically remarked :

> "In old times a single cane contained enough juice to fill a pot; but now that the king has taken to unjust ways, one stalk of sugarcane yields juice only just enough to fill a cup."

Then the king gave up the project he had formed to plunder a rich merchant. Numerous passages in the inscriptions as well as the Prabandhas, already quoted and to be quoted may lead the modern man to conclude that Bhōja was extraordinarily vain and was pleased with silly flattery. It has already been pointed out that the praises of the king by his courtiers and others were not intended to be understood literally nor were they so, but were couched in conventional language. Indeed even today the conventions of certain religious sects require that when two men talked to each other, each should call the other a 'god' (*dēva*) and himself a slave (*dāsa*). Like the English words 'thanks' these are but dead locutions, mechanically repeated and meaning nothing. Such specimens of conventional politeness ought to be considered along with the words used when, as already quoted, the poorest of the poor unhesitatingly scolded kings for their evil deeds. The latter alone show the actual relations between the kings and their subjects. How freely courtiers spoke out their minds to kings without fear of royal displeasure is illustrated by the following incidents.

Dhanapāla was a Jaina and therefore had a great regard for the sanctity of life, not only human but also animal. Once when the king went out hunting, he pierced a deer with an arrow and looked at the face of Dhanapāla, expecting an appropriate *ślōka* of praise for his skill as a hunter. But the *ślōka* that issued from the poet's lips was to the following effect :—

> "Your valour in hunting deserves but a place in the region of hell ;
> It's evil as policy ; he who takes refuge is always held guiltless ;
> That the weak one is slain by the mighty is always a matter for sorrow,
> Oh ! Woe worth the day when this happens, it shows that the world is then kingless."

The king became indignant that he got a reproach when he expected a compliment and cried,

> "What is the meaning of this ?"

But the answer came,

> "Even foes who take grass in their mouths are reprieved from sentence of death ;
> Can you slay these most innocent beasts who have always green grass in their mouths ?"

Then a great pity rose in the heart of the king and he resolved to break his bow and throw away his arrows and to renounce the sinful habit of hunting for the term of his natural life.

Dhanapāla being a Jaina condemned Vedic sacrifices as being against the law of *ahiṁsā*, but Bhōja being a Vaidika Kṣattriya patronized them.

Once the king while in the company of Dhanapāla, heard the plaintive cry of a goat which was fastened to a *yūpa*, (sacrificial post), in the *yajñaśālā*, (house of sacrifice) and he asked the poet,

> "What does the animal say?"

Dhanapāla replied,

> "It is entreating not to be slain. It says I am not desirous of enjoying the fruits of heaven, I never asked you for them; I am always satisfied with eating grass; this conduct does not become you, holy man."

He then added,—

> "Having made a sacrificial post, having slain beasts, having made gory mire, if by this one goes to heaven, by what does one go to hell? Truth is my sacrificial post, penance indeed is my fire, deeds are my fuel, one should offer harmlessness as a burnt-offering, thus one's sacrifice is approved by the good."

Such was the utter want of fanaticism in ancient times, that the king heard this vigorous condemnation of his religious beliefs without anger.

Dhanapāla even went so far as to ridicule the gods whom Bhōja worshipped, without ruffling his temper. Dhanapāla once visited a temple in the company of his master, and there noticed statues of the God of Love and of his wife, Ratī. The poet then laughed, and sang,—

> "Throughout the world is Śiva famed for self-restraint but yet
> For fear of parting makes Umā a part of his own self;
> 'Does Kāma want to conquer us?' he says and pats her hand
> With his and o'er this God of Love he triumphs laughingly.
> Sky-clothed he is; why then has he a bow? if he sports a bow,
> Why then is he besmeared with ash? If daubed with holy ash,
> How is it then he has a wife? and if he has a wife,

How comes it that he is said to hate the mighty God of
Love?
Beholding thus his master's inconsistent conduct, Bhṛṅgī,
Is worn down to a skeleton and covered with network of
veins."

On another occasion Dhanapāla ridiculed the worship of the cow, which was practised by Bhōja and the majority of his subjects,—

" She feeds on human filth, she does not show
Discernment in her love, she weds her son,
She smites all creatures with her hoofs and horns,
What good in her does make you worship her?
Is it because she gives you milk? So does
The buffalo. No better is the cow."

There is no reason to doubt the authenticity of these stories. They show that according to the ideas of the time, the royal throne was not isolated by the atmosphere of divinity and kings behaved like ordinary men to all their subjects. Bhōja's affability, his heroism and his unstinted charity moved Śītā, a cook by profession, to seek his audience and sing,

" His valour has ruined the race of his enemies,
His glory has filled the wide vessel of earth,
His bounty has reached all the wants of petitioners,
As earth does extend to the shores of the great sea,
His faith it does mount to the feet of the husband
Of Pārvatī, daughter of the lord of the mountain."

CHAPTER VII

BHŌJA, THE SCHOLAR AND THE PATRON OF SCHOLARS

Saṁskṛta literature had had an unbroken course of evolution for several thousand years before Bhōja mounted his throne in the early years of the XIth century. Ages of inspiration had alternated with ages of criticism more than once. The lovely poetry of the Vedic mantras with their direct contact with Nature had been followed by the criticism, lower and higher, of the *Brāhmaṇas* and the *Vēdāngas*, the sublime spiritual flights of the *Upuniṣads*, by the analytic expositions of the *Sūtras*, the first and the best *Kāvya*, the *Rāmāyana*, and the Great rambling Epic, forming the two *Itihāsas* and the Dramas of Bhāsa and other early playwrights, and the *Buddhacarita* of Aśvaghoṣa, by the earlier *Alankāra* works, which have been mostly absorbed in later text-books of criticism, till the swan-song of inspired Saṁskṛta literature issued from the lips of Kālidāsa. Even before Kālidāsa's time inspiration was supplanted by ingenuity, poetic images derived from an observation of the phenomena of Nature and springing unconsciously in perfect poetic form from the deepest depths of the poet's soul, had given way to the endless play of ready but conscious wit and the coinage of images by unbridled fancy; tricks of language, to music of verse, in short, poetic style to *estilo culto*. Even honey palls after a time and the over-cloyed taste has to be whipped up by smarting pepper. The age of Śūdraka and Viśakhadatta and Kālidāsa must needs be followed by that of Subandhu, Bāna and Māgha. Composition came to be loaded with ornament, just as in architecture the unity and symmetry that characterized the earliest structures were concealed in later ones by the wealth of decorative detail. Meanwhile, the rhetoricians, Bhāmaha and Daṇḍī, among others, instead of being camp-followers in the army of poets, became the directors of the march of poetry. Then came Anandavarddhana, who made the doctrine of *Dhvani* reach a premier place in the field of poetry and taught that the essence of poetry consisted not in style nor in sentiment, but in subtle suggestion by tone. The net result of all these is that from Bhōja's time a new form of poetry became predominant, where emotion was less important than ingenious play on words, where fantastic conceits predominated over poetic images, and the sound became as important as the sense, and the technique of poetry as important as its matter and commentaries stifled the thought of the original writer and the exposition of science usurped the place of the appeal to the emotions. Bhōja is said to have composed 104 poems to match with the 104 temples he built. Of these 28 have been discovered. Perhaps 104 is a mere formal number indicating 'very many'. The books that have been so far found, arranged according to the subjects they treat of are :—

I. *Astronomy and Astrology*

(1) Rājamārttāṇḍa
(2) Rājamṛgāṅka
(3) Vidvajjanavallabha (praśnajñāna)
(4) Ādityapratāpasiddhānta

II. *Medicine*

(5) Āyurvēda Sarvasvam
(6) Viśrāntavidyāvinoda
(7) Sālihotra (a Veterinary Manual)

III. *Śilpaśāstra*

(8) Samarāṅgaṇaśūtradhāra

IV. *Grammar*

(9) Śabdānuśāsanam

V. *Philosophy*

(10) Rājamārttaṇḍa (Vedânta)
(11) ,, (a com. on Patañjali's Yoga Sutras)
(12) Tatvaprakāśa (Śaivaism).
(13) Siddhāntasaṅgraha, ,,
(14) Śivatatvaratna Kālika ,,
(15) Yukti Kalpataru ,,

VI. *Dharma Śāstra*

(16) Vyavahārasamuccaya.
(17) Cārucaryā.

VII. *Arthaśāstra*

(18) Cāṇakyanīti (Daṇḍanīti) and Putramārtāṇḍa.

VIII. *Alaṅkâra*

(19) Sarasvati Kaṇṭhābharaṇa
(20) Śṛṅgāraprakāśa.

IX. *Poetry and Prose.*

(21) Rāmāyaṇa campu.
(22) Vidyāvínōdakāvyam.
(23, 24) Two Prākṛt poems (lately discovered at Dhār).
(25) Mahākālivijayam (a stotra)
(26) Sṛñgāramañjari (prose tales)
(27) Subhāṣitaprabandha.

X. *Lexicography*

(28) Nāmamālikā.

A list in the *Prabhāvaka Caritra* (c. 1450 A. D.) names a good many more works.[1] It has been suggested that one man, and that a king who was engaged in many wars, could not have found time to write so many works. Hindu scholars can easily understand how this is easily possible. In India, from boyhood scholars are trained to carry all books they read in their memory, so that when they in their turn begin to write books they need not spread on their tables all the books that they have learnt on the subject. Drawing from the inexhaustible stores of memory, they can write new books especially on the Śāstras at a rate so fast that the foreigner cannot understand their speed of composition.

Moreover, Bhōja founded at Dhārā his famous university called the temple of Sarasvatī, where lived a host of scholars who must have helped Bhōja in his literary activity.

But it is not by the number of his works that Bhōja is remembered by posterity but by his daily intercourse with scholars and by the play of wit and the flow of poetic images that characterized his daily literary Darbars.

The forging of poetic images constituted the chief intellectual enjoyment of Bhōja and his coteries of scholars. Some of the stories, not all, relating to these are anachronistic, but, genuine or not, they are highly interesting. A few examples may be given. One night a certain thief cut a tunnel beneath the wall of the palace and entered the treasure-room where the king was sleeping. The king suddenly awoke at the midnight hour and seeing the moon recently risen in the sky, "like the rising of his literary sea," there arose from his lips this half-stanza,—

---

[1] Ep. Ind. i. p. 231.

> "What appears on the body of the moon like a strip of cloud
> They assert is a hare but I think it doesn't wear that form."

The thief replied,—

> "But I think that the moon has its body well marked with the brands of a hundred scars
> Of the meteor-strokes of the side-looks of the maidens who are parted from the foes you have killed."

The thief was rewarded by the king very generously for this exceedingly fine piece of poetic flattery. There is nothing very improbable in the story, for some thieves of ancient India were so learned that treatises on the art of thieving composed by them are mentioned in Saṁskṛta literature. Indeed one such book was attributed to the God Kārttikēya.

On another occasion the porter at the door of the king's audience-chamber reported that the family of Sarasvatī, consisting of a father, mother, son, daughter and a wretched one-eyed maid-servant, all learned, were waiting at the gate, eager for an interview with the king. They were admitted and the king gave to the father this quarter-couplet to complete :—

> "From unsubstantial things a man should substance draw."

The man replied,—

> "Munificence from wealth, and truth from speech, and fame and piety from life,
> Doing good from one's own body, from unsubstantial things a man should substance draw."

To the son the king gave the following to complete,—

> "Himālaya, in truth, the king of hills
> Mēnā, afflicted with bereavements made."

Immediately the son replied,—

> " By thy great valour's fire was melted down
> Himālaya, in truth the king of hills;
> Mēnā, afflicted by bereavement, made
> A bed of shoots the refuge of her body."

To the matron the king propounded the riddle,—

> " Which am I to feed with milk ? "

She replied,—

> " When Rāvaṇa, truly, was born with ten mouths, and one body,
> His mother was wondering which am I to feed with milk."

To the share of the maid-servant fell the following quarter-couplet :—

> " On whose neck am I to hang ? "

She replied,—

> " A certain lady, angered with neglect
> Did drive away from home her wretched spouse,
> My friend, then in my mind arose this thought
> Hereafter, 'on whose neck am I to hang' ?"

The king rewarded them all but he did not test the daughter. At the next audience everyone was allowed to be present, and the king was walking up and down with an umbrella held in the hand, when the porter reminded him of the daughter's presence. He said, 'speak' and she uttered this stanza,—

> " O Bhōj, crest-jewel of kings, the light of your race,
> Thou holdest thy umbrella even at night ;
> Lest your face should make the moon abashed with shame,
> And chaste Arundhatī become unchaste."

The king straightway took her to wife.

Another lady who won her way to the king's heart by means of her poetic talents was Vijayā, daughter of Śītā, the cook. When the rays of the moon fell through the lattice upon the King, she exclaimed,

" O planet adorned with a spot, pray stop this sport,
Of touching human beings with thy light rays
Thou art not fit for touching, because thou art
Remains, of the adornment of the spouse of Caṇḍī."

On one occasion when the king was going round on his daily circuit, he happened to reach the bank of the river. Then he saw a Brāhmaṇa, fording the river with a load of firewood on his head. The king accosted him with the hemistich,—

" How deep is the water, O Brāhmaṇa ? "

The Brāhmaṇa completed the line with,—

" O king, it is knee-deep."

The king continued,—

" How were you reduced to this state ? "

The Brāhmaṇa replied,—

" Not everywhere are there patrons like you,"

all the phrases put together forming one *ślōka.* The king gave a large present to the impecunious Brāhmaṇa and dismissed him. On a subsequent occasion when the king, seated on the royal elephant, was going round the town on his daily circuit, he noticed that a certain beggar was picking up grains of rice that had fallen on the ground. Bhōja then uttered a half-stanza,—

" What's the use of people being born who can't fill their own stomachs ? "

The beggar finished the stanza with—

" There's no use of people being born, who don't help others though well able."

The king retorted,—

" O mother, don't give birth to a son who's intent on begging from neighbours ! "

The beggar added,—

" Do not, O Earth, give support to those who refuse the requests of their neighbours ! "

The beggar had been prevented by the chief men of the town from obtaining an entry into the king's audience-hall and resorted to this trick to interview the king and benefit by his generosity.

This display of poetic repartee became part of diplomatic conversations also. Once Bhōja placed in the hands of a *Sandhi vigraha* (lit.), minister of peace and war, the following couplet and sent it to his rival, Bhīma of Gujarāt,—

> "The lion who easily cleaves the stout foreheads of elephants whose valorous progress
> Is published abroad doesn't war with the deer and yet cannot be said to have peace with him."

Soon came the reply,—

> "By destiny Bhīma on the earth was created destroyer of the sons of Andhaka.
> He minded not hundreds of foes, can he care for you who are but one such?"

Bhōja was naturally proud of the learning and poetic skill of the pandits of his country and contemptuous of those of Gujarāt. One day he remarked to the Gujarātī consul at his court,

> "Not one of your most famous scholars is fit to be weighed in the balance with a cowherd of my land."

Bhīma heard of this boastful speech and sent to Bhōja a learned man disguised as a cowherd and also a *hetaera*. When the cowherd was taken to the royal presence, he said,—

> "Bhōja, tell me, is it proper, on your neck you wear this jewel,[1]
> Parting Lakṣmī on your breast and Vānī dwelling in your mouth?"

The king was immensely pleased and then turned to the *hetaera*, and noticing that the collyrium which she had daubed at the outer corners of her eyes, reached up to her ears, asked her,

[1] Sarasvatīkaṇṭābharaṇa.

"Why here?" She replied, "They are asking". The face of the king beamed with joy at the reply and he ordered a large sum of money to be presented to her. The courtiers were surprised at the magnitude of the reward; then the king said,—

> "Observing that the collyrium applied to her eyelids extended from the outer corners of her eyes to her ears, I asked her 'why here'? She divined my meaning immediately and replied that her eyes had gone disguised as collyrium-streaks to her ears and were asking whether I was the very king Bhōja that the ears had previously heard about."

The completion of half-stanzas is a form of poetic exercise which has always been a kind of amusement in India and is even now an important item in the programme of learned assemblies. It is said that Bhōja was daily surrounded by a hundred scholars who were skilled in this kind of impromptu poetic composition. The best example of this is the following. While a certain short poem was being read in the royal presence by some pandits, they came upon the following half-stanza,—

> 'Alas! indeed the fruits of former deeds
> Are terrible in the case of living men."

More than a hundred clever pandits attempted to complete the *ślōka*, but failed in the contest. Then Dhanapāla said,—

> "Alas! Alas! those very beads which gleamed
> On Siva's head are rolled about by kites."

This Dhanapāla was mentioned in a previous chapter, as boldly criticizing the king and his religious beliefs and practices. But when seated in the Darbār he could turn a compliment as neatly as any other courtier. Thus,—

> "The creator wished, O Dhārā Lord, to count the earthly kings,
> Then made a streak in the sky with a piece of chalk to note you down,

The streak became this stream divine, for none can equal you.
He let the chalk drop down; and it became Himālayās."

The other pandits criticized the stanza as reeking with exaggeration. Then Dhanapāla retorted,

"Vālmīki makes the sea to be bridged with the rocks that were brought by the monkeys and Vyāsa by the arrows of Arjuna; and yet they are not charged with exaggeration."

Being a great scholar and a skilful poet himself, the stream of Bhōja's magnificent generosity was generally directed to poets, especially those who were witty. The poets of the period believed that their poverty was due to remissness of kings in the matter of the patronage of learning. On one occasion a poverty-stricken poet, on being taken by the porter to the royal presence, said,—

"The mother is displeased with me and also with her son's wife;
The wife of the son mislikes her husband's mother and also me;
I am displeased with both this woman and also with the other;
O king, do solve this riddle, whose is the fault that has this caused?"

The king recognized the justice of the rebuke conveyed by means of this doggerel and ordered a handsome present to be given to the poet. On another occasion, the king promised to give a poet a large reward for every stanza he composed, but the poet kept up pouring such a continuous poetic flood that the king exhausted his resources rewarding him and had to entreat him to stop. This story may have a deep tinge of exaggeration, but it gives us a good picture of the lavish way in which Rājaput princes kept up the old Indian tradition of the royal encouragement of poetic skill. Hence, one of the *praśastis* (eulogistic poems), of the Paramāra royal house says that

> "Bhōjarāja was a jewel without a rival, (a hero) who caused the best men to tremble. He, who resembled King Pṛthu, possessed the earth up to Kailāsa, up to the Malaya hills, and up to the two mountains of the setting and the rising sun; he scattered in (all) directions the weighty crowd of the supporters of the earth, easily uprooting them with the shaft of his bow, and giving highest joy to the earth. He accomplished, ordered, gave and knew what (was) not (in the power) of anybody else; what other praise can be given to illustrious Bhōja, the poet-king."[1]

[1] E. I. i. pp. 237–8.

CHAPTER VIII

BHŌJA'S DEATH

The last great rival of Bhōja was Karṇa, son of Gāṅgēyadēva, lord of the Cēdi country. He was inspired by unbridled ambition and the desire to attain to the supreme status of the overlord of India, such as Bhōja enjoyed. So he

> "honoured the quarters with the pearls from the frontal globes of the majestic elephants of his enemies, cleft by his sword."[1]

He found soon that the three Kaliṅgas, which adjoined his dominions were in a disorganized state and boldly proclaimed himself *Trikaliṅgādhipati*, the Lord of the three Kaliṅgas. His fame spread throughout the country, so that

> "the Pāṇḍya relinquished violence, the Murala gave up his arrogant bearing, the Kuṅga entered the path of the good, the Vaṅga trembled (along) with the Kaliṅga, the Kīra stayed at home like a parrot in the cage, (and) the Hūṇa left off being merry."[2]

It will be noticed that only very minor princes of the middle of the XIth century are mentioned, and the Cālukya, or the Sōlaṅki or the Paramāra, are not here referred to. The Pāṇḍya was then the vassal of the Śōḷa, so, too, the Kuṅga, the chief of Koṅgumaṇḍalam; the Kīra was a petty ruler, subordinate to the kings of Kāśmīr. Later, when Bhīma of Gujarāt was dead and the first Śōḷa empire had begun to decline and that of the Pālas to flicker, it was claimed that Karṇa was

---

[1] Ep. Ind. ii. p. 6.

[2] *Ib.* ii. p. 15.

> "waited upon by the Cōḍa, Kuṅga, Huṇa, Gauḍa, Gurjara and Kīra princes." [1]

Absurd tales were told about the birth of Karṇa. His mother Dāmatī by name, was a mistress of magic and delayed the hour of his nativity by her magical arts to an hour when the benign planets were in the signs of the Zodiac that contained their exaltation (*ucca*) and were at the same time in the first, fourth, seventh and tenth houses, which are called centres, and the malign planets in the third, sixth and eleventh houses. Because he was born in such an auspicious moment, he conquered the circle of the regions, he was obeyed by 'one-hundred and thirty-six kings', he became master of the 'four royal sciences'[2] and was praised by Vidyāpati and other poets thus,—

> "In the forest, on the face of the wives of thy foes destiny has hung the heavy necklace, (or heavy loss, *hāra*), on their two eyes the heavy bracelet (or drops of tears, *kaṅkaṇa*), on the hips bestowed the ornamental tattoo (or a row of leaves for dress), and on the two hands the (red) patch (the *tilaka* tree). Why has this strange style of adornment befallen them? Having abandoned the breast of Viṣṇu too much engrossed with the *gōpīs*, Lakṣmī, the goddess of fortune, resides in your eyes, mistaking them, I think, for lotuses. Since, O fortunate king Karṇa, wherever goes the spray of your eyebrow, wavy like the creeper, there is broken the seal of poverty, brittle through fear".

Such flattery acted as a spur to his ambition.

One day he sent this message to Bhōja by the mouth of an ambassador,

> "In your city there are 104 temples built by your orders, and even so many in number are your poetical compositions, and so many are your titles: therefore conquer me in a battle with a force of four arms (elephants,)

---

[1] Ind. Ant. xviii. p. 215.

[2] The triple veda, logic and metaphysics, the science of government and practical arts.

chariots, cavalry and infantry), or in single combat, or as a disputant in the four sciences, or in munificence, and become the possessor of 105 titles; otherwise, by conquering you, I shall become the lord of 137 kings."

King Bhōja had now become old, and weak; he was weary of wars, and indeed of all earthy vanities. So, he offered Karṇa this competition in temple-building,—

"I in Avanti and Karṇa in Kāśī, shall, on the same day and at the same moment, select the sites of two temples fifty cubits in height, and begin to build them, running them in rivalry with one another, and on whichever king's temple the Kalaśa (finial of the spire) and the flag shall fitly be set up, on that day of festival, the rival king must abandon his umbrella and cowries (symbols of royalty)."

Karṇa succeeded in finishing his temple before Bhōja's was completed. Probably the temple that Karṇa erected in this contest was the golden temple called Karṇa's *Mēru.*

At this time Bhōja was attacked by the malady to which he succumbed in a few months. While he was still stretched on the bed of sickness, Karṇa entered into a league with Bhīma for making war with Bhōja, invited him to attack Mālva in the rear, while he himself was leading an army into it from Benares, and promised him half of Bhōja's kingdom. It was no more a case of fighting for showing off one's personal prowess, but one due to earth-hunger. Bhōja, ill as he was, had all the mountain passes and fords leading to Mālva closed up, so that his enemies could not penetrate into the province. Their armies remained idle beyond the borders, awaiting a favourable opportunity. Then Ḍāmara, Bhīma's agent at Dhārā, sent through one of his servants to his master at Aṇahilavāḍ the following cryptic message,—

The fruit of the mango is fully mature,
The stalk it does hang by is loose and the wind,
It blows so strong, the branch is decayed,
The end of the business who can foretell ?

King Bhīma read the riddle aright and the two princes were biding their time.

In 1055, the icy hand of death began to creep over Bhōja's body. He performed the duties prescribed in the śāstras as appropriate to the occasion. He then ordered,—

" After my death my hands ought to be placed outside the chariot which will carry my corpse and the following stanza recited,

" Whose hand is this, O wife and son,
Whose hand, O all my house ?
Alone I came, alone I go,
With nothing on my hands and feet." [1]

The people repeated this stanza all through the town. It then reached the ears of Karṇa and he boldly broke the fortifications of Dhārā and captured the city. Bhīma thereupon demanded from Karṇa half of Bhōja's wealth as his share and was given the revenues from all temples of Śiva, Viṣṇu and Gaṇēsa in the kingdom. On account of this the King of Gujarāt was eulogized as follows :—

" Śrī Bhīmadēva, though terrible (*bhīma*) to his foes, ever granted enjoyments to his friends, (and) as ruler carried this load of earth. What wonder was there that his horses, supremely skilled in accomplishing the five paces (called *dhārā*) quickly gained Dhārā, the capital of the Emperor of Mālva." [2]

The death of Bhōja was bemoaned by means of a number of elegies. One *praśasti* refers to the event in these terms :—

[1] Literally, 'having rubbed' them, so that nothing belonging to the earth, not even dust, might stick to them and be taken away by the dead man.

[2] E.I. i. p. 302.

"When that devotee of Bharga whose brilliance resembled that of the sun, had gone to the mansion of the gods, the earth, like Dhārā, was filled with dense darkness, his foes and his hereditary warriors became infirm in body." [1]

Bilhaṇa, though attached to a rival court, mourned the death of Bhōja in these touching terms,—

"Bhōja was the lord of the earth, and not, indeed, comparable to vulgar kings. Woe is me! Dhārā cried to him (i.e. Bilhaṇa) through the voice of the pigeons nesting on the lofty towers of her gates, 'why dids't thou not come into his (Bhōja's) presence.'" [2]

An anonymous eulogy says,—

"When the cloud of your hand had begun its ascent
In the heavenly quarters, benignant ten,
And was raining the nectar-like flow of wealth,
Like the lightning did flicker your bracelet of gold
And the river of your fame then began to swell high,
Quite refreshed were all virtues as well as the earth;
The wide lake of petitioners filled, and the fire
Of poets that were poverty-stricken was well quenched;
Like the wishing-tree, thy munificent gifts
They did frighten all poverty away from the world.
Like incarnate Bṛhaspati did he compose
His victorious works, in a very short time;
In Rādhāvēdhā, like Arjuna.
The immortals quite speedily summoned the king,
By his glory their hearts were compelled to wish
For his presence; and soon to heaven he went.

An inscription of Devapāla, dated 1228, has it,—

"There was a king, great like Kaṁsa's conqueror, an ornament of the Paramāra family, the glorious Bhōjadēva, who occupied the surface of the earth by the van of his army. When the lustre of the moonlight of his glory overflowed the lap of the regions, there closed the day lotuses of the glory accumulated by hostile kings." [3]

---

[1] E.I. i. p. 238.

[2] Bil. Vik. Car. xviii, 96.

[3] E. I. ix. pp. 113-4.

Bhōja left such deep imprints on the sands of time that he became the one great Indian Emperor remembered by prince and peasant alike even up to day. Devarāya of Vijayagaram felt it the greatest honour possible to be compared to Bhōja in *bhōga* (enjoyment, *i.e.* proper use of wealth (*bhōgē bhōjamiva*).[1] In the XIIIth Century the Hoysalas of Mysore struck a wedge between the Śōla and the Pāndiya territories by founding a capital at Kaṇṇanūr in the Trichinopoly District, and building a temple called Hoysalēśvara temple. The name in Tamil became *Poysalēśvara*, and then *Pōsalēśvara*. The common people around, in time, forgot the Hoysalēśvara dynasty as they did many another dynasty; but all people remembered Bhōja (Tamil Bōja) and so to-day the temple is called the Bōjēśvara temple and legend has it that Bhōja lived half the year in his capital and the other half *incognito* in Southern India and built this temple.

---

[1] Numerous similar comparisons are found in South Indian vernacular poems dating from the XVth century.

CHAPTER IX

SOCIAL AND RELIGIOUS LIFE IN THE TIMES OF BHŌJA

Social life in India has not much changed since Vedic times. Many of the customs referred to in the mantras of the Vēdas can still be observed unchanged especially in the villages. Not so the religious life of the people. Luckily, the social and religious life of the people in the age of King Bhōja have been described by an impartial and well-informed foreigner who resided in India during that period.

Abū Raiḥān Muḥammad Ibn Aḥmad Al Bērūnī was a councillor of the Prince of Khwārizm (Chorasmia, now Khīva) and, when Maḥmūd annexed the province, was taken as a hostage to Ghaznī (1017). He was permitted to live in India and being a learned *munajjim* (astrologer-astronomer), he was attracted by the Indian treatment of his favourite subject, mastered Sanskrit and Sanskrit lore, and wrote his *Indika*. He was one of the earliest and most accurate foreign scholars of Indian books and his book, containing quotations from thirty Sanskrit books, is a very valuable account of the Indian culture of the XIth Century. He was very much attracted by Indian philosophy, especially by the *Bhagavad Gītā* which he quotes frequently; but when he has to condemn Indian customs, he does so without shrinking.

> "They are by nature niggardly in communicating that which they know, and they take the greatest possible care to withhold it from men of another caste among their own people, still much more, of course, from any foreigner."[1]

[1] A.-I. i. p. 22.

His fairness is proved by the following statement.

> "The Hindus believe with regard to God that he is one, eternal, without beginning and end, acting by free-will, almighty, all-wise, living, giving life, ruling, preserving; one who in his sovereignty is unique, beyond all likeness and unlikeness, and that he does not resemble anything nor does anything resemble him."[1]

Modern customs with regard to eating prevailed in his days.

> "Since it is forbidden to eat the remains of a meal, every single man must have his food for himself; for if any one of the party who are eating should take the food from one and the same plate, that which remains in the plate becomes, after the first eater has taken part, to him who wants to take as the second, the remains of the meal, and such is forbidden."[2]

After describing the castes, the author points out that

> "according to some, only the Brāhmaṇa and Kṣatriya are capable of [attaining to liberation], since the others cannot learn the Veda, while according to the Hindu philosophers, liberation is common to all castes and to the whole human race, if their intention of obtaining it is perfect."[3]

Thus by the Xth Century, the Vedantic restriction of Sanyāsa and Mokṣa to Brāhmaṇas had generally given way before the Āgama extension of it to all men. Al Bērūnī is so unprejudiced as to point out, after an elaborate account of idols,

> "that such idols are erected only for uneducated low-class people of little understanding; that the Hindus never made an idol of any supernatural being, much less of God; and . . . how the crowd is kept in thraldom by all kinds of priestly tricks and deceits."[4]

After pointing out that "it was in China that paper was first manufactured" and that "Chinese prisoners introduced the fabrication of paper into

[1] A.-I. i. p. 27.
[2] *Ib.* i. p. 102.
[3] A.-I. i. p. 104.
[4] *Ib.* i. p 122.

Samarkand and thereupon it was made in various places, he says, that in South India they wrote on leaves "of a slender tree like the date and cocoanut palms" called *tāla* (palmyra) and "bind a book of these leaves together by a cord on which they are arranged, the cord going through all the leaves by a hole in the middle of each," and

> "in Central and North India people used the bark of the *tūz* tree, one kind of which is used as a cover for bows. It is called *bhūrja*. They take a piece one yard long and as broad as the outstretched fingers of the hand, or somewhat less, and prepare it in various ways. They oil and polish it so as to make it hard and smooth, and then they write on it. The proper order of the single leaves is marked by numbers. The whole book is wrapped up in a piece of cloth and fastened between tablets of the same size. Such a book is called *pūthī* (*pusta*, *pustaka*). Their letters and whatever they have to write, they write on the bark of the *tūz* tree." [1]

There were in the author's days eleven different scripts used in India from the *Siddhamātrka* of Kāśmīr to *Dirwari* (*Drāviḍi*) of the Tamil country.

> "The Hindus begin their books with *ōn*, meaning thereby a confession of the unity of God." [2]

Al Bērūnī notes that in his days the Hindus alone went

> "beyond the thousand in their numeral system", "at least in their arithmetical technical terms", and "extend the names of the orders of numbers until the 18th order for religious reasons, the mathematicians being assisted by the grammarians with all kinds of etymologies." [3]

Certain Hindu customs struck him as strange and he describes them in a manner which will strike the Hindu reader as curious.

> "The Hindus eat singly, one by one, on a table cloth of [cow] dung. They do not make use of the remainder of a meal, and the plates from which they have eaten

---

[1] A.-I. i. p. 171. [2] A.-I. i. p. 173. [3] A.-I. i. p. 174.

are thrown away if they are earthen. They have red teeth in consequence of chewing areca-nuts with betel-leaves and chalk. They drink wine before having eaten anything, then they take their meal. They sip the stall of cows (*gōmūtra*), but they do not eat their meat. They beat the cymbals with a stick. They use turbans for trousers. Those who want little dress are content to dress in a rag of two-fingers' breath, which they bind over their loins with two cords; but those who like much dress, wear trousers lined with as much cotton as would suffice to make a number of counterpanes and saddle-rugs. These trousers have no (visible) openings, and they are so huge that the feet are not visible. The string by which these trousers are fastened is at the back. Their *Sidar* (a piece of dress covering the head and the upper part of breast and neck) is similar to the trousers, being also fastened at the back by buttons. The lappets of the *Kurtakas* (short shirts from the shoulders to the middle of the body with sleeves, a female dress) have slashes both on the right and left sides . . . On festive days they besmear their bodies with dung (ashes?) instead of perfumes. The men use articles of female dress; they use cosmetics, wear ear-rings, arm-rings, golden seal-rings on the ring-finger, as well as on the toes of the feet . . . . They ride without a saddle, but if they put on a saddle, they mount the horse from the right side . . . . They wear a girdle called *yajñopavīta*, passing from the left shoulder to the right side of the breast . . . . They do not ask permission to enter a house, but when they leave it they ask permission to do so. In their meetings they sit cross-legged. They spit out and blow their noses without any respect for the elder ones present, and they crack their lice [fingers?] before them. They consider the *crepitus ventris* as a good omen, sneezing as a bad omen. ; . .

They use black tablets for the children in school, and write upon them along the long side, not the broad side, writing with a white material from the left to the right. . . . They write the title of a book at the end of it, not the beginning."[1]

"In a country where not the whole spot in the house which is prepared for people to eat upon it is plastered with clay, where they, on the contrary, prepare a

[1] A.-I. i. pp. 180–2.

separate table cloth for each person eating by pouring water over a spot and plastering it with the dung of cows, the shape of the Brahman's table-cloth must be square."[1]

A man who performs a pilgrimage

"sets off to wander to some holy region, to some much venerated idol, or to some of the holy rivers. He worships in them, worships the idol, makes presents to it, recites many hymns and prayers, fasts, and gives alms to the Brāhmaṇs, the priests, and others. He shaves the hair of his head and beard, and returns home."[2]

"In every place to which some particular holiness is ascribed, the Hindus construct ponds intended for the ablutions. In this they have attained to a very high degree of art . . . . They build them of great stones of an enormous bulk, joined to each other by sharp and strong cramp-irons, in the form of steps (or terraces) like so many ledges; and these terraces run all round the pond, reaching to a height of more than a man's stature."[3]

"It is obligatory with them [the Hindus] every day to give alms as much as possible. They do not let money become a year or a month old, for this would be a draft on an unknown future, of which a man does not know whether he reaches it or not. With regard to that which he earns by the crops or from the cattle, he is bound to pay to the ruler of the country the tax which attaches to the soil or the pasture-ground [ground rent?]. Further, he pays him one-sixth of the income in recognition of the protection which he affords to the subjects, their property, and their families. The same obligation rests also on the common people, but they will always lie and cheat in the declarations about their property. Further trading businesses, too, pay a tribute for the same reason. Only the Brāhmaṇs are exempt from all these taxes."[4]

"The Hindus marry at a very young age; therefore the parents arrange the marriage for their sons."[5]

---

[1] A.-I. ii. p. 135.

[2] *Ib.* ii. p. 142.

[3] A.-I. ii. p. 144.

[4] *Ib.* ii. p. 149.

[5] A.-I. ii. p. 154.

"If a wife loses her husband by death, she cannot marry another man. She has only to choose between two things—either to remain a widow as long as she lives or to burn herself." [1]

"The judge demands from the suitor a document written against the accused person in a well-known writing which is thought suitable for writs of the kind and in the document the well-established proof of the justice of the suit. In case there is no written document, the contest is settled by means of witnesses without a written document." [2]

Among other festivals of the people the following are described by Al Bērūnī:—the *Hindoli caitra*, when the image of Vāsudēva is swung in a cradle, *Yajñas* for five days before the full moon in *Vaiśākha*, the *Vasanta* on the day of the vernal equinox, that on the first of *Jyaiṣṭha*, when first-fruits of all seeds are thrown on water, the full-moon day of *Śravaṇa* when Brāhmaṇs are fed, the *Mahānavami*, on the 8th Āśvayuja when the moon is in the station *Mūla*, the *pitṛpakṣa* in *Bhādrapadā*, the first *Kārtīka* called the *Dībālī*, when they light a great number of lamps, and on the 16th *Phālguna*, the *Sivarātri*, and the *Sankrāntis*, i.e., the days of the equinoxes and the solstices. These extracts from the *Indika* prove that the claim of Hindus that their *dharma*, i.e., religious, social and political institutions have been *Sanātana*, essentially unaltered from very early times is true, that the ordinances of the *Śāstras* were not merely theoretical rules, but were actually practised, and that the cause of early marriages was not the advent of Muhammadans, as is so often asserted, but they prevailed before the Muslim conquest of the land. Though most of the Kṣattriya princes of North India were Śaivas, Al Bērūnī's account of Indian religion gives us the

[1] A.-I. ii. p. 155.

[2] *Ib.* ii. p. 158.

impression that Viṣṇu-worship was universal in India; from this we can infer that a wave of the Vaiṣṇava religion spread over India at the time. Buddhism was practically dead, Al Bērūnī knows almost nothing of the religion or its literature.

But Al Bērūnī was intimately acquainted with the life of the people only in Sindh and Gandhāra. Besides Viṣṇu temples those of Śiva and Sūrya abounded in India in the days of Bhōja. The worship of Brahmā was not neglected even in Sindh, for an image of Brahmā in bronze, three feet two inches high with four shaven faces with a *mālā* (rosary) in one of his two hands, discovered in Sindh, shows that in this age, as in later times, temples of the first of the *Trimūrti* existed but very rarely.[1]

The Paramāras were Vaiṣṇavas; they employed the Garuḍa banner; but in North India in Bhōja's days and before and after, there did not prevail the fanatic hatred of Śiva by the Vaiṣṇavas and of Viṣṇu by the Śaivas, such as has been the leading note of religion in South India since the Xth Century onwards. Therefore we find the Paramāras praising both Śiva and Viṣṇu in their inscriptions. The Jaina cult, fully organized into a church consisting of ascetics and laymen, became popular in Central India from the IXth Century. A legend current about Bhōja's assembly of scholars throws light on the friendly relations that prevailed among the votaries of different sects in those days. The king held a *sabhā* of paṇḍits representing all sects and asked them what was the true way of salvation. Each spoke in favour of the sect to which he belonged; and it was resolved finally that they should propitiate the goddess Sarasvatī for six months and

[1] A. S. p. 11.

thus find out the true way. At the end of the period, on a certain night, Sarasvatī manifested herself to them and said,—

> You must listen to the Dharma of the Bauddhas, you must practise that of the Jainas, in daily life you must observe that of the Vedas, you must meditate on the supreme Śiva;

She then vanished from their view. The goddess meant that all these religions taught the same Dharma, but the Bauddha exposition of the Dharma was the clearest, the Vedas taught how that Dharma could be practised in the daily life of the common man, the Jainas prescribed best the path of asceticism for him who had renounced the world, but all should meditate on the supreme God to reach the goal. The *sabhā* of paṇḍits summed this up as their final decision on the true way in these words!

> "Religion is characterised by harmlessness; one must honour the goddess Sarasvatī. By meditation one obtains salvation; this is the view of all the sectaries."

Brāhmaṇas, poets and others migrated to Dhārā in expectation of royal presents. By a copperplate grant, dated the 3rd *tithi* of the dark fortnight of Māgha in 1022 A. D., the village of Vīrāṇaka to the west of Nāgadraha was given by Bhōja to Dhanapati Bhaṭṭa, son of Govinda Bhaṭṭa of the Āśvalāyana Śākhā of the Āgastya gōtra who had migrated from Śrīvāḍe.[1] The inscriptions of this period present us with the picture of Brāhmaṇas constantly immigrating from one part of India to others.

[1] I.-A. vi. p. 49.

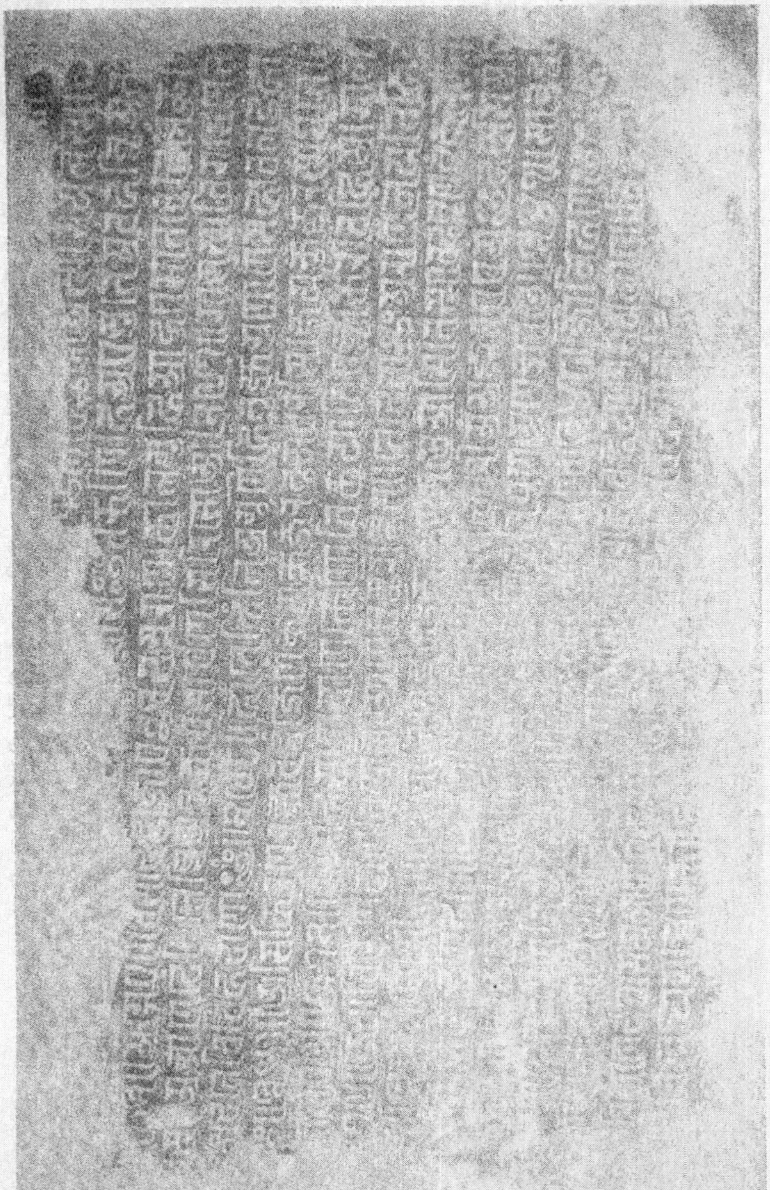

CHAPTER X

BHŌJA'S MONUMENTS

Bhōja is said to have built 104 temples; an inscription says,

> "He made the world (*Jagatī*, which means also 'a site for buildings) worthy of its name by covering it all round with temples, dedicated to Kēdārēśvara, Rāmēśvara, Sōmanātha, Suṇḍira, Kāla, Anala and Rudra." [1]

His temples have all been destroyed by the hands of time, of renovators and of iconoclastic Mussulmans.

The most famous of these temples was the one built at Dhārā and dedicated to Sarasvatī, wherein was located the great university founded by Bhōja. In it was enshrined the figure of Sarasvatī, a minified photographic copy of which is the frontispiece of this book.

> "It is a *chef d'oeuvre* of rare beauty, in its exquisite serenity of pose, in its entrancing and balancing rhythm, in the elegance and suavity of its aquiline features, and in the general restraint in the treatment of the anatomy which is almost wholly free from any exaggeration."

Its general affiliation with Śōḷa sculptures of the period and partial resemblance to the contemporary Pāla and Orissan sculptures show that Indian art has been essentially one throughout the country, while a comparison with the figures shows the steady, continuous evolution of Indian art throughout the ages. An inscription on the pedestal, dated 1035 A. D., as translated tentatively by Mr. K. N. Dikshit of the Archaeological Survey, runs as follows :—

> "Om, the Vidyādharī of the town Bhōja, the moon among kings, having first made the mother goddess of speech . . . . great in fruit, created the auspicious image. This was made by Manabhala, the son of the craftsman Sahira, written by Śivadēva in the Samvat Year 1091."

---

[1] Ep. Ind. i. p. 238.

Our image presents besides some unique features.

> "She is conceived with four hands, having a rosary, a book, a vīṇā or a kamandalu or a goad, and the "expounding gesture (*vyākhyāna mudrā*). She wears . . . . the holy thread and the breast-bands (*Kucabandha*)."

She wears pearl garlands; her face is 'serene' (*Saumya mukhī*) and her form lovely (*cāru-rūpinī*). A *Muni* is represented by the bearded figure in a corner. The figure mounted on a lion is Pārvatī.[1]

Bhōja had, besides, a round tank constructed at Kapālēśvara in Kāśmīr,

> "with heaps of gold that he sent. He had vowed that he would always wash his face in water from [this], the *Pāpasūdana tīrtha*"

and Padmarāja, a betel-seller and favourite of the contemporary Kāśmīrī king, Ananta,

> "made the fulfilment of his [i.e. Bhōjā's] difficult vow [possible] by regularly despatching from this [*tīrtha*] large numbers of glass jars filled with that water." [2]

Remains

> "of the enclosure . . . [which] Bhōja constructed among this sacred spring [are still extant]. The latter now rises in a circular tank of at least 60 yards in diameter, which is enclosed by a solid stone wall, and by steps leading to the water . . . From the formation of the ground, it is evident that this tank has been formed by closing artificially the gully in which the spring rises on the hill side." [3]

An iron pillar has recently been found at Dhārā. Most likely it belongs to Bhōja's time when the arts flourished. Probably Kulacandra, after returning

---

[1] Vide *Rūpam*, No. 17, Jan. 1924, pp. 1–2.

[2] Rājataraṅgiṇi, viii. 190–3.

[3] *Ib.* (Stein's note).

from Aṇahilvāḍa, set up an iron pillar to celebrate his victory. At least three portions of a broken iron pillar are lying at Dhārā.

The pillar, when entire, was of a total length of 43 feet 4 inches and an average width of 10¼ inches each way.

> "The longest portion measures 24 feet 3 inches, and is square in section throughout; the second 11 feet 7 inches of which 8 feet 6 inches is square and 3 feet 1 inch of octagonal section; and the third piece, 7 feet 6 inches in length, and, with the exception of a circular collar at the end, about 8 inches deep, is of octagonal section throughout. . . . [There are] a number of small holes at intervals in its sides, varying in depth from 1¾ to 3 inches, and in diameter about 1¼". They run up each of the four sides of the square shaft and the corresponding faces of the octagon . . . The holes in all probability were made, as the mass of the pillar was built up in order to hold the ends of crowbars or levers with which the workmen could better handle and roll over the great heavy column as bit by bit of semi-molten metal was added and welded on to the white hot stump of the shaft. The crowbars were removed and shifted from place to place as required: one stuck and was chipped off, leaving the end in the hole." [1]

The pillar was probably topped by a Garuḍa, the figure of which was engraved on the seals of Bhōja and other Paramāras. There is no means of deciding with certainty whether the iron pillar was set up on Kulacandra's return from Aṇahilvāḍa or when Arjunavarmā, a descendant of Bhōja, invaded Gujarāt a century later and laid it waste. It is a unique pillar of victory and was probably erected by Bhōja to commemorate his victory over Bhīma, who was almost as great a warrior and a patron of the arts of peace as Bhōja. Three pieces of the pillar have been recovered and perhaps there still lies somewhere concealed a fourth piece and the total length of the original piece was probably fifty feet.

---

[1] A. S. R. 1902-3, pp. 205-7.

The Muhammadan rulers of Mālva in the 15th Century destroyed the temples with which Bhōja beautified Dhārā and used the materials for new structures of their own, like the Lāṭ Masjīd, outside which lies one of the portions of the iron column already described. In its neighbourhood there is the mosque of Kamāl Maulā,

> "where not only pillars and building stones from Hindu temples one of which was known to the inhabitants as Rājā Bhōja's School, probably his famous Śāradā temple where a university was located by him have been utilized, but a large portion of the flooring of the praying chamber is paved with black marble slabs, formerly covered with Sanskrit inscriptions; and even the lining of the *Mihrab* itself was, by a fortunate chance, found to consist of similar slabs, in this case with the engraved faces merely turned inwards and the inscriptions thereon unharmed."[1]

The story of the "fortunate chance" is this:

> "At the angle of junction of the side and black wall of the *Mihrab* are some holes long enough to admit a hand and arm, and it was entirely owing to the fortunate chance of some one passing his hand through one of these apertures and discovering letters on the back surface of the stones that the existence of the inscriptions was revealed. The method employed to obtain a record of these inaccessible inscriptions is also worth telling. Partial impressions were taken in the first instance by an ingenious system of paper rolled round jointed rods which were inserted through the apertures into the space behind the wall, and then unrolled; the impression was then made by rubbing lampblack upon a pad fixed to the extremity of a similar rod. This process was, of course extremely laborious but was deemed well-paid by the results, so long at least, as there appeared no chance of removing the stones."[2]

Since then, the slabs were removed from the structure. They were found to contain two long inscriptions and several fragments. One of them consists of two odes to the tortoise incarnations of

---

[1] A. S. R. 1903-04, p. 44.

[2] *Ib.* 1902-03, p. 18.

Miḥrāb of the Kamāl Maulā Mosque, Dhār.

Viṣṇu, called *Avani kūrmmaśatakam*, written in Māhārāṣṭrī Prākṛta and in the Aryā metre. The substance of the first ode is to the effect that no body has carried the earth as well as the tortoise and no mother is so happy and worthy of praise as the mother of this tortoise. In the second it is said that even the tortoise has been surpassed by King Bhōja who now carries the earth.

The two odes claim to be Bhōja's compositions. The first says,

> "Even to the tortoise rest has been granted by King Bhōja alone. By him this *Kūrmma Śataka* has been composed after he had taken away all hope from the enemies." [1]

The second has it,

> "By whom the chief of mountains, (nay) all the mountains here (on earth) have been reduced in weight, by this King Bhōja has this *Śataka* been composed." [2]

Bhōja is in the second ode several times directly addressed, but this and the self-praise implied by his authorship, though repugnant to modern manners, was allowed by the conventions of society in those days and were not taken literally as the modern man would do. Of the fragments "all that can be said at present is that in all probability they belong to odes to Bhōja of vast dimensions" and probably contained strings of verses in praise of the bow (*kōdaṇḍa*) of Bhōja.[3]

The grammatical serpentine inscriptions, though actually incised a little after Bhōja's time, repre-

---

[1] A. S. R. 1902-03, p. 18.

[2] E. I. viii p. 242.

[3] A. S. R. 1903-04, pp. 239-40.

sents the initial grammatical teaching imparted in Bhōja's Sarasvatī Temple. Among other things they show that the *Kātantra* treatise on grammar supplanted Pāṇini in North India from the Ist century A. D., till it was revived in Benares in the XVIIth century. The following account of these serpentine inscriptions is entirely taken from a note on the subject by Mr. K. K. Lele, History Officer of Dhār State.

There are two Sanskrit grammatical inscriptions, in the Nāgarī characters, on two stone pillars in the mosque near the tomb of Moulāna Kamāluddīn at Dhār. The mosque is still popularly called Bhōja Rājā Ki Nisal or Rājā Bhōja's College. This corroborates the fact that the mosque was built on the site of Rājā Bhōja's College, held in a spacious and splendid temple of Sarasvatī, the Goddess of Learning and Arts, discovered in the same mosque in 1902. There is ample evidence to show that the mosque was built not only with the materials of the temple, but on the very site of it. The existence of numerous mutilated large Nāgarī inscriptions on the pavement and of a part of the plinth of the original temple with a Gō-Mukha on the north-east corner proves the fact beyond doubt. Moreover, the image itself of Sarasvatī (Goddess of Learning) recording its installation in the temple by Rājā Bhōja himself in Samvat 1091 (A. D. 1035) exists in the British museum and its facsimile has been published in *Rūpam* (No. 17, January, 1924, Calcutta) (and reproduced as the frontispiece of this book).

The two pillars bearing the inscriptions are among those that support the dome of the prayer hall, one on each side of the raised pulpit. The one near the pulpit containing the Sanskrit alphabet faces the east;

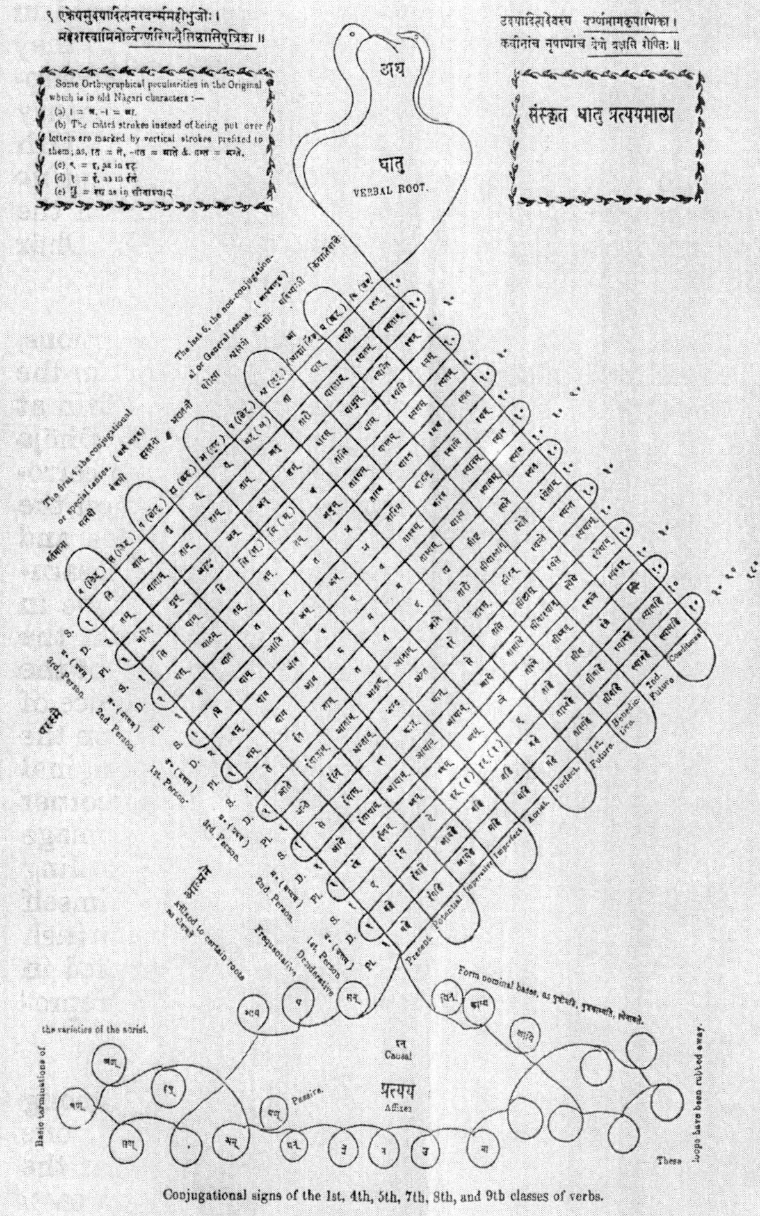

Conjugational signs of the 1st, 4th, 5th, 7th, 8th, and 9th classes of verbs.

Two snake grammatical Inscription.

वर्ण माला.

* In the original अ is represented by । and आ by -।

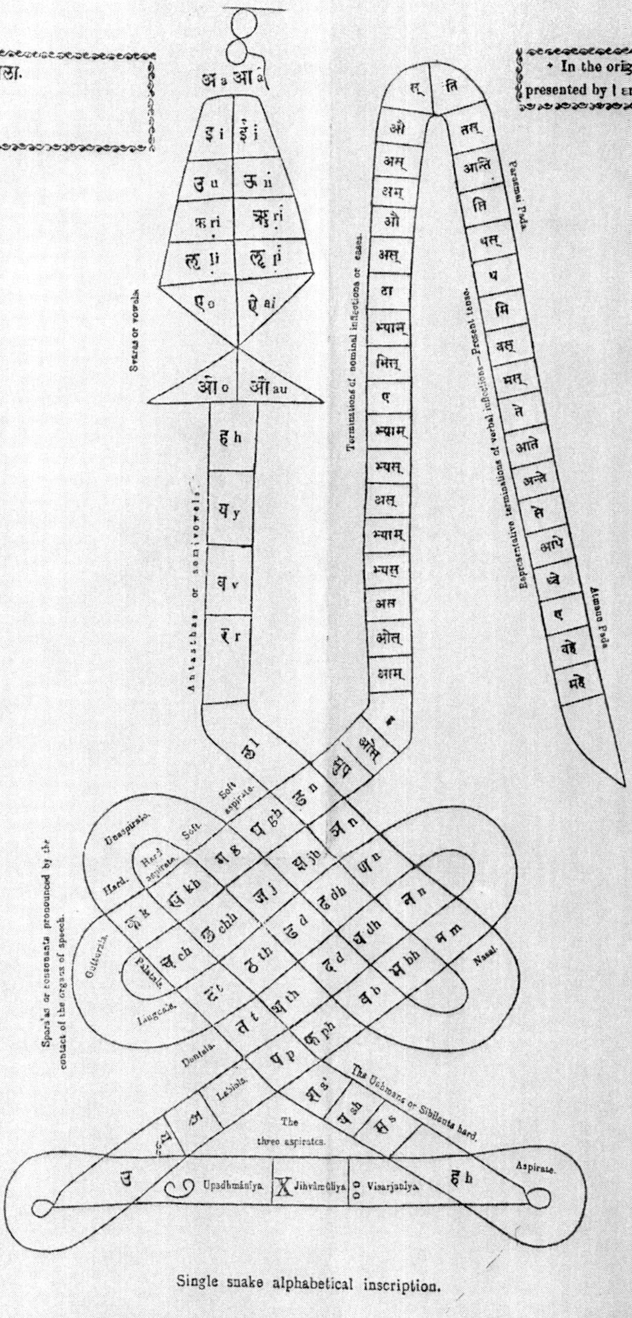

Single snake alphabetical inscription.

The other, at a distance from the pulpit to the south, contains the Sanskrit verbal terminations, facing the south with two Sanskrit verses inscribed over it containing the names of the two successors of Rājā Bhōja.

The inscriptions have been called Sarpa Bandhas because the letters and terminations are inscribed in the oblong open spaces formed by the twisting of serpents length-wise and cross-wise. The tables are ingenious in design and beautiful and mysterious in appearance. The pillars being of gray limestone unsuited for engraving have undergone partial decay in some places. The surface has been cut through by lines which have deformed some of the letters. The right corner of the base of one of the inscriptions has altogether disappeared. Most of the other numerous Nāgarī inscriptions lying in this building were engraved on durable black stone slabs. Many of them were used for the pavement of the central prayer hall with their inscriptions erased, while those that have been recently discovered, whether full or fragmentary have their inscriptions intact. The pillar inscriptions are also tolerably well preserved. Probably their inconspicuous position has saved them from the fate which other inscriptions in this building have undergone at the hands of ignorant fanatics. These inscriptions are called grammatical because they deal with grammatical matters. One of them contains a chart of classified Saṁskṛta alphabet and the other, tables of verbal conjugational terminations like similar illustrations in a modern school. The alphabetical chart is made up by the windings of one serpent only. It contains the Saṁskṛta alphabet in Nāgarī character of the XIth or XIIth century A. D. and the chief inflectional terminations of nouns and verbs. The former are given in classes in the body of the serpent and the latter in the tail. The consonants do not differ much from those in common use now, but the vowels have quite different shapes. The letters of the alphabet are more than half an inch in length and breadth, while those of the terminations in the tail are much smaller. The whole inscription is 2 feet and 3 inches in height and one foot in breadth. There are altogether 55 letters and symbols, and 21 nominal and 18 verbal inflectional terminations. As the alphabet plays the chief part in this inscription, it is called Alphabetical. The first letter at the top is probably the letter क्ष (Ksha) which is the last but one letter in the usual serial order of the Sanskrit alphabet ज्ञ (jna) being the last. It is placed at the top and with the first letter अ (A) it probably indicates the अक्षमाला or Indian rosary. The letters begin with vowels and end with the three Visarags (aspirates) Visarajanīya, Jihvā Mūliya and Upadhmāniya. It is not known why the first two vowels अ (a) and आ (ā) are not given in full. So also the object of giving ऋ, यु and उ in the left hand side of the triangular base is not clearly seen.

The table of verbal terminations is bigger in size being 2½ feet in height by 1½ feet in breadth. It is made up by the intertwining of two serpents probably a male and a female one. It contains chiefly the 18 personal terminations of the ten tenses and moods, of classical Saṁskṛta verbs (excepting only the Vaidika लेट्) arranged in columns. There are three numbers in Sanskrit, and two sets of terminations (Parasmai pada and Atmanē pada) for each of the tenses and moods; so for the three persons in each, there are altogether 180 terminations, ninety of each set as shown under:—

	Parasmai pada.			Atmanē pada.		
3rd. P.	Sing.	Dual.	Pl.	Sing.	Dual.	Pl.
2nd. P.	,,	,,	,,	,,	,,	,,
1st. P.	,,	,,	,,	,,	,,	,,

Total 9 + 9 = 18

Grand total for ten tenses = 180

Thus there are altogether 18×10=180 verbal terminations, 90 of each set, given in the table. They are duly numbered on the right hand side and are arranged in slanting columns from the left to the right, and are given in the spaces, left between the zigzag cross turnings of the serpents. The two sets of terminations (Parasmai and Atmanē), the three persons (the 3rd or Prathama, the 2nd or Madhyama and the 1st or Uttama) and three numbers (Singular, Dual and Plural) are noted on the eft hand side in order. The names of the tenses and moods are marked at the top of the columns by the initial letter of each. They are as under :—

Initials	Full name	Pāṇini's name	English name.
1. व	वर्तमाना	1 लट्	Present.
2. स	सप्तमी (7th)	7 लिङ्	Potential.
3. प	पंचमी (5th)	5 लोट्	Imperative.
4. ह्य	ह्यस्तनी	6 लङ्	Imperfect.
5. अ	अद्यतनी	8 लुङ्	Aorist.
6. प	परोक्षा	2 लिट्	Perfect.
7. श्व	श्वस्तनी	3 लुट्	1st Future
8. आ	आशीः	9 आशीर्लिङ्	Benedictive.
9. भ	भविष्यन्ती	4 लृट्	2nd Future.
10. क्रि	क्रियातिपत्तिः	10 लृङ्	Conditional.

Besides the primitive basis, Sanskrit verbs have several derivative bases showing causality, desire, intensity, etc. These and other details are indicated in the round loops in the triangular base below the principal table of terminations. The heading of the inscription is अथधातु प्रत्यय (याः) of which the words "अथधातु" stand between the heads of the serpents and the last word प्रत्यय straight down in the base. The letters in this inscription are smaller and therefore, in several places somewhat indistinct.

The names of the tenses and the details given in the base are not taken from the Great Sanskrit Grammarian Pānini, cir. 500 B.C. They are taken from the Kātantra (also called Kalāpa or Kaumàra) —a small manual of Sanskrit Grammar, which appears to have been specially prepared in order to simplify the subject in 1st century A. D., which became very popular in North India for a long time.

This grammar is still a text-book in Bengal and was so much in use in old times in other places from Kāśmīr in the north to Mahārāṣṭra in the south and has taken such deep root in the soil, that a few early sutras (formulas) of it are still learnt by heart, in every indigenous Vernacular School of Malva, Gujarāt and other parts of India, under the name of Sidhā. Every child's first lesson begins with Sidhā ; but in the mouth of unlettered Pāṇḍyas (Pedagogues) and their ruder pupils the text has been so corrupted that it can now be hardly recognised to be Saṁskṛta. For illustration three or four corruptions are quoted below :—

सीधो यरणा, समामुनाया, चत्रे चत्रे दीसा दौ सथेरा.

The correct sutras (aphorisms) of Kātantra run thus :—सिद्धोवर्णसमाम्नायः ॥१॥ तत्र चतुर्दशादौ स्वराः ॥२॥

Above this table and over the heads of the serpents, there are engraved two Sanskrit stanzas of the Anuṣṭubh Metre. These supply important historical data and raise the inscription, from a mere grammatical curiosity to the status of a valuable historical document. The stanzas indicate the period to which they belong ; they confirm the tradition about Bhōja Sālā or Bhōja's School and indicate the site of Bhōja's School.

I. In the first couplet occur the names of Udayāditya and Naravarmā, (father and son), in the second, that of Udayāditya alone.

Now Udayāditya and Naravarmā were the almost immediate successors of the famous Rājā Bhōja, who ruled at Dhār during the 1st half of the 11th century and whose name, as a scholar, writer and great patron of scholars and writers, has become a household word in India. They, therefore, must have reigned at the end of the XIth and the beginning of the XIIth century A.D. Hence the two stanzas in question, cannot be, in all probability, less than 800 years old. The grammatical tables themselves may perhaps be older still. The mosqué in which these inscriptions are now found was built by Sultan Mahmūd Sha Khilji of Māṇḍu about 861 Hijri or 1457 A.D. as can be seen from the Persian inscription on the gate-way leading to the tomb.

II and III—Both the serpentine pillar inscriptions being grammatical are of educational interest and must have been designed by some ingenious teacher and permanently engraved on the pillars as charts in modern Schools. They may also have some mystical or occult meaning.

The two Sanskrit stanzas at the top read as under in modern Nāgari :—

एकेयमुदयादित्यनरवर्म महीभुजोः ॥

महेश स्वामिनोर्वर्णास्थित्यै सिद्धासिपुत्रिका ॥ १ ॥

उदयादित्य देवस्य वर्णनागकृपाणिका ॥

कवीनांच नृपाणांच वेषो वक्षसि रोपितः ॥ २ ॥

Purport.

(1) This Sword of Kings Udayāditya and Naravarmā, the worshippers of Śiva, was ready equally for the protection of the (four) Varṇas (classes of society) and of the Varṇas or alphabet (meaning learning).

(2) This serpentine Sword of King Udayāditya intended for the protection of letters (learning) and social classes has been set up as a badge for the breasts of poets (scholars) and kings (Rulers).

But the most wonderful of Bhōja's constructions was the Bhōjpur Lake,[1] a feat of hydraulic engineering forgotten by all till its ancient bed was recovered with great pains by Kincaid. The lake spread on the valley of Betwa to the extent of 250 square miles.

The holy Bētwa in its upper reaches sweeps round hills, glides down broad valleys and races down narrow glens and the region round has been the focus of religious and commercial activities since the days of Gautama, the Buddha. Here the first Bauddha Ācāryas preached and wrote their books. It seems Bhōja was stricken with an unsightly skin disease and in those days, as is done by Indians even to-day, it was diagnosed as a kind of leprosy. Bhōja's doctors could not cure it and, as Indian Rājās always did, he resorted to a holy Sanyāsī for advice. The sanyāsī prescribed that the king should construct a lake, larger than any other in India, and fed by 365 springs, one for every day in the year, and bathe in it at a specially chosen auspicious hour. The Royal Engineers set about to discover a proper site for the construction of the lake, and after long, tedious and expensive search,

[1] Ind. Ant. xvii. pp. 348–52 on which this account is based.

found it in the region of the head-waters of the Bētwa, 20 miles from where Bhōpāl now stands. Here was an extensive valley hemmed in by a ring of hills and in the hill-wall, there were only two breaks, one a little more than a hundred and the other about 500 yards wide. Bhōja's engineers spanned them by two wonderful dams, each consisting of a bund with an earthen core, faced on the inner and outer sides with immense blocks of stone. The skill of the artisans of the period can be judged from the fact that the blocks were laid, one on the other without mortar, but yet their edges fitted so truly that the bund was absolutely water-tight. It is needless to add that the faces of the bund sloped inwards from the base. The greater bund was about 40 feet high and 100 feet broad on the top on which runs to-day a part of the road from Bhōpāl to Kaliakheri.

But when the streams that flowed into the valley were counted, it was found that they were only 359. The engineers cast about for means to bring up the streams to the mystic number 365 that were wanted by the sage; then a chief of the Gonds, who then (as now) inhabited this bit of the Daṇḍaka forest pointed out another stream near, which was fed by six hill-springs. The chief's name was Kaliya and the grateful engineers called the river Kaliasot. But the Kaliasot which could increase the drainage area of the lake by about 500 square miles, flowed outside the well-enclosed valley which was to be the bed of the proposed lake. To utilise the waters of the Kaliasot, the engineers built near Bhōpāl twenty miles off, a magnificent cyclopean dam, constructed exactly like the other two, but immensely broad for its length and height. Thus was created a storage tank from which the surplus

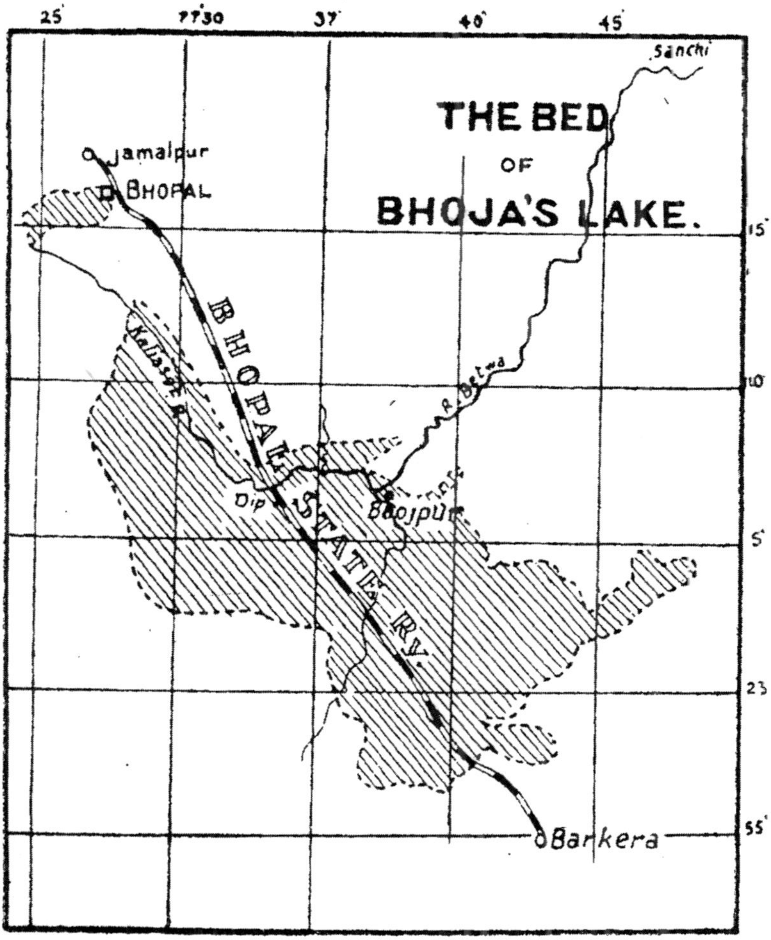

THE BED
OF
BHOJA'S LAKE.
25'
77 30
37'
40'
45'
15'
10
5'
23
55'
Sanchi
Jamalpur
BHOPAL
BHOPAL STATE RY.
Kaliasot R.
R. Betwa
Dip
Bhojpur
Barkera

waters could feed the lake during the three dry months that succeeded the rains; from here "the river ran at right angles to its former course round the hills into the Bētwa valley and became a most valuable feeder to the constructors of the great lake, because it carried the surplus waters of the great lake into the larger lake." The greater dam was so constructed as to turn the Kaliasot into the Bētwa and from the top of the bund the old bend of the Kaliasot can even now be seen. The bund itself is now so covered with jungle as to be invisible unless when very carefully scrutinised.

Thus was created the Bhōjpur lake, in its days the largest and the most beautiful lake that adorned the surface of India, presenting to the view "one unbroken sheet of water, except where islands added to its beauty". It was in places a hundred feet deep and on all sides surrounded by high hills. It was provided with a waste weir by means of "a cutting through the solid rocks of one of the lower hills on the east side". "It is at the blunt a pex of a triangular valley opening from near the great dam, and is probably two miles from it in a direct line. Its position so far from the dam affords another proof of the practical ability of the Hindu engineers of the time; for any error in the levels would have quickly destroyed the dam which, though stone faced on both sides, was filled in by earth and could not long have withstood an overflow. There are signs on its rocky and unbroken sides which show that high water-mark was within six feet of its top." The water weir is now buried in impenetrable jungle and was accidentally discovered by Col. Kincaid. When the waste weir valley was accessible a visit to it at the close of the rains would have been well worth making, for there could be seen the overflow falling down in broken cascades to the Bētwa 100 feet below, and could be heard the waterfall roaring like thunder. The lake was a broad sheet of sweet water, refreshing alike to the eyes dried, and the lips parched, by the hot winds. From the broad bosom of the lake peeped now and again green islands relieving the monotony of the view; the village of Dīp (from Sanskrit Dvīpa, island) standing on a small hill and now a station on the Bhōpāl State Railway, testifies to the fact that it was in Bhōja's time an island two miles in length spread on a hill standing in the borders of the Bhojpur lake. In those days trees like the pippal whose ever-trembling leaves shiver the rays of the sun into ever-moving dots of light, grew all around the lake; the ears were charmed by the shrill chirping of birds overhead and the gentle lapping of little waves at the feet. Here and there the jungle was cleared, breaking the verdure which clothed the hills round the lake and ran right down to the water's edge and towns were built. One such town built first below the waste weir was Bhōjpur where more than one group of large flat stones mark the sites of Bhōja's boat-houses. In that ruined city are the remains of a temple celebrated for its gigantic polished quartzite lingam. Not far from the northern end of the lake was built Bhōpāl, Bhōja's pāla (bund) on which nestles the ancient fort to the west of the modern city; the fort is on the brink of the storage tank already described and is filled with remains of Jaina temples and the fine sculptures that characterise them. Beyond the western shore away on the mountains rose the powerfully-built fort of Gōnār defended by a deep dike cut out of the solid rock. Every morning Bhōja would sail on boats across the lake and leaving them in the boat-house, would inspect the fort or visit the temples on the other shore and return to his palace for his mid-day meal. The vast watery plain cooled the atmosphere all round for several miles and held up the water so that the river Bētwa was never in floods. Bhilsa and other towns rose below the flood level of the river and they enjoyed immunity from inundation which they do not to-day, for this wonderful piece of ancient Hindu engineering was destroyed by Shāh Hussain, the greatest of the Māṇḍu Sultans, a little more than 400 years after it was built. He coveted the fertile land which formed the silt-covered bed of the lake for agricultural purposes and ordered the smaller of the dams to be broken. It required an army of labourers to work for three months to destroy it and three years elapsed before the lake was emptied of its waters and thirty before the bed became dry enough for human habitation; but Shāh Hussain did not live to see the consummation of his hopes. Then numerous little towns arose which now stud the valley where the lake existed; round the towns green wheat waves where the cool waters once rolled and the line of the Bhōpal State Railway runs where Bhōja's pleasure boats sailed in the breeze, and India's sons pass across the bed of the lake on which sailed their forefathers of nine centuries ago, ignorant of the history of the site, notwithstanding the silent testimony of the great bund, the ruined temples and the large stone pillars of Bhōja's boat-house past which they are hauled by the railway engines snorting with a speed unknown to Bhōja's boats which once silently slid along. Human eyes stare unintelligent on the jungle which has grown all round, the verdant hills stand grimly looking on and laughing at the mutations of human ambitions.

Bhōja was the *beau ideal* of his time in the matter of military heroism, patronage of poetry and other fine arts, as well as of the useful arts. Modern Indian princes exhibit their prowess not on the field of battle, but only on those of cricket or football or polo but have otherwise kept up the ancient virtues. They and also modern princes of Industry and Commerce still emulate Bhōja in the founding of centres of learning and the erection of temples, larger and more ornate than those of the Lord of Dhārā, and in thus helping the ancient culture of India to keep growing on from more to more.

INDEX

By T. V. Mahalingam, M.A.

D

E

G

H